All Mimes Must Die!

All Mimes Must Die!

The Best of
"We Recommend"

Skewed-view Essays from
The Memphis Flyer

TIM SAMPSON

Contemporary Media, Inc.
Memphis, Tennessee

Library of Congress Catalog Number: 95-83106

All materials appearing herein were originally published in
The Memphis Flyer.

ISBN 0-9649821-0-2

Produced by Contemporary Media, Inc.
Illustrations by Jeanne Seagle

Contemporary Media, Inc.
460 Tennessee Street
Memphis, Tennessee 38103

Manufactured in the United States of America

5   4   3   2   1

for

My Very Wonderful Family

and for

Hal, Leonard, Sandra, John

and

Dot

Acknowledgments

I'd first like to thank Kenneth Neill for making this book possible, and for helping me get out of town and sometimes out of the country when he could see that I wasn't long for the mental institution. For their help in producing this book, I'd like to thank Cheryl Bader, James Haley, Michael Finger, Elizabeth Burr, Janae Sholtz, Molly Zanone, Beth Beard, Sarah McVoy, Sarah Hall, Lennie Hearns, Marilyn Sadler, Catherine Cuellar, Bruce VanWyngarden, and Ciara Neill. Thanks to Jeanne Seagle for her wonderful art, and to John Burton Tigrett for his preface. Also, thanks to Judy Short, Kyle Parish, Kevin Henson, Mark Gardino, Barclay Roberts, Mark Jones, Lynn Sutter, Tom Smith, Jerry and Leasa Swift, Brantley Ellzey, Jim Renfrow, Linda Gail Lewis, Wendy Moten, Mary Ann Eagle, Carol Ricossa, Stan Carter, Sarah Gratz Land, Linda Willis, Sally Goodwin, Brian Roper, Linda Prudhomme, Tony Beall, Ron Diaz, John McKinney, Jesús and Lisa Cudemus, Adele Balton, Collier Black, and, for being nutty enough to give me my first writing job and then teaching me how to do it, Ed Weathers.

Table of Contents

Introduction

by Kenneth Neill

"We Recommend" made its debut in the second-ever issue of the *The Memphis Flyer*, on February 23, 1989. Hard as it may be to imagine today, the column in its infancy was nothing to laugh about. For the first few months, "We Recommend" was pretty much your standard weekly "best bets" column, written by the newspaper's overworked founding editor. It was downright serious.

But as time passed, Tim began to lose it. We shouldn't have been surprised. Here, after all, was a man who takes absolutely nothing in the world seriously, including, above all else, himself. Here we were, asking this chronic curmudgeon to write cogently and "respectfully" about the coming week's events, in Memphis, Tennessee, of all places. We should have known what would happen. It was a little bit like casting Roseanne Barr to play the lead in *Gone With the Wind*.

By the end of that first summer, Tim had "lightened up," to put it mildly. "We Recommend" wasn't shaping up as your average rah-rah listings column. ("It's a good thing the rest of the week is packed," he wrote of one July Tuesday, "because tonight is deadsville.") And Tim had begun fine-tuning the mantra for which he is now justly famous, the mantra that's been the grand finale of nearly every "We Recommend" column since he first used it while previewing Elvis International Tribute Week that August:

"All I can say is, go. Just go... If that doesn't sound good enough to check out, if you're some kind of snot-nose who finds Death Week tasteless, or if you're just some kind of fat slug who never leaves the house and wouldn't even go out to see Priscilla model one of the wigs Elvis bought her, then just stay home. Do whatever you like, because I don't care. I don't even know you, nor do I want to know you, and besides, I've got to blow this dump to get home and iron my jumpsuit."

The rest, as they say, is history. "We Recommend" has now appeared hundreds of times in our pages, and Tim Sampson just may be the most popular columnist in Memphis. One thing is certain; whenever the *Flyer* conducts readership surveys, people invariably vote "We Recommend" their favorite *Flyer* column by an overwhelming margin.

I won't even try to explain the essence of Tim Sampson's humor. If you're familiar with his work, then you well know what's ahead of you in the next hundred pages or so. If you're not, all I can say is that you'd better fasten your seatbelt, and leave your prejudices and predilections behind. And if you can't take a joke, please, put this book down right now, and buy something else.

Happily, *The Memphis Flyer* is now nearly seven years old, and for better or worse a well-established feature of weekly Memphis life. Its founding editor has now moved onto bigger if not better things; since 1992, he's been editor of *Memphis* magazine, our sister publication. In that role, he's helped revitalize *Memphis* as it approaches its twentieth birthday.

For a brief moment, Tim considered giving up "We Recommend" when he moved over to the magazine. As if he had a choice. We laughed heartily, all the while capitulating to the exorbitant salary request Tim thought surely would guarantee the column's extinction.

No such luck. Now he'll probably want even more dough, being a book author and all. We might even have to take up a collection. But, hey, that's the least we should do for the guy. After all, it's not every day that a column no one else wanted turns into a genuine civic treasure. Thanks, Tim, for making us all laugh, more times than we can even remember.

Kenneth Neill
Publisher
The Memphis Flyer
October 1995

Preface

By John Burton Tigrett

The only true love of my long life was a small blonde girl named Pearl White. I was 12 years old at the time. We met every Saturday morning at the Plaza Theater in Cleveland, Mississippi, where — big spender that I was — I had paid ten cents for a front-row seat. Our romance had only one small problem. Pearl lived in disasters. As we parted each week she was either desperately holding on to a small bush — that you could plainly see was slowly coming out of the ground and about to plunge her into a great chasm several hundred feet below — or a giant saw was bearing down on her while she was firmly tied to a moving belt — or a locomotive engine belching enormous puffs of smoke was...it became endless. Then as the screen went dark, there I was on the edge of my seat, with only seven days left until the next serial to figure out how I was going to save...my love.

The only person who has surpassed dear Pearl for mishaps, calamities, tragedies, misfortunes, and plain old daily trouble is Tim Sampson.

Every Wednesday morning as I break off another fingernail trying to get in the nearest beat-up, handleless, green tin box for a free copy of *The Memphis Flyer*, I start to smile. What possible misadventure would his column tell us happened to him this week? Had he been run down and was prisoner of a grocery cart, pushed by an overly large woman who'd used too many food stamps — or had he been sleepwalking again and ended up napping with his head in the wrong end of the bathtub? His surprises and disasters never stop!

But whatever cloud of despair he is under at the moment, you will find it to be a very, very funny cloud. For Tim Sampson is one of the few truly talented humorists writing today. His unique catastrophes are pure joy, his daily tragedies are always good for at least two belly laughs. And in one of these wonderful misfortunes — if you look closely — you may see a reflection of one of your own!

John Burton Tigrett
September 1995

All Mimes Must Die!

April 14–20, 1994

Hush, Hush, Sweet Anus

I am bored to death. You can only watch Talk Soup so many times before you begin feeling like a freak yourself. More of one than usual. So there's nothing left to do but pace. I've already unsuccessfully flipped through all the television channels looking for the guy singing the country-western song about the myriad pleasures of the laxative Doxidan, which, says the commercial, you should take in the P.M. for a B.M. in the A.M. I have even resorted to new cat-costume games, and my cat, Jeff, is none too happy about having gauze wrapped around her head while we're playing car-wreck kitty. Nor was she very delighted when I made her wear one of those pieces of cardboard that comes in the collar of a new shirt: flying-nun kitty. No wonder I keep finding her buried in the back of the closet. I keep telling her she needs to come out of the closet, but she just looks at me like I'm crazy. Go figure. I'm also already bored with spring. I'm really sick of walking around my yard and imagining what it would look like if I planted flowers and killed all the weeds and trimmed the hedges and picked up all the litter. The imagination can only do so much. Besides, I might miss the Funyun bag that's been sticking out of the top of the bush next to my front door since last summer. So I guess it's back to picking on people. Let's see. How about that Kimberly Mays, the teenager who was switched at birth and ended up with the wrong parents and then went to court and hogged the national press when she decided she wanted to fix it so that her natural parents could never contact her again, and then ran away from the parents she'd been living with all her life and went to live with her natural parents. Maybe if one of her sets of parents had popped her jaws a little more often, she wouldn't be such an insufferable brat. Maybe she ought to

be caned. Anyway, I'm already bored with even talking about her. Where is Tonya Harding when we really need her? Let's see. There's old Harry Blackmun retiring from the Supreme Court, leaving open a spot to be filled by the Clinton administration. Now that it's made up of a mix of men and women, Jews and gentiles, blacks and whites, I think they ought to appoint a midget. They're always getting the short end of the stick. I know people who hate midgets. *Hate* them. I, personally, have no aversions to midgets, though I have disturbing dreams about them. Of course, I also dreamed the other night that I was in a roomful of people, including Jacqueline Kennedy Onassis, and when someone asked her a tacky, embarrassing question about how much money she had, I broke the ice by changing the subject to the many uses of garlic cloves. And here's one for the shrinks: She asked me if I had my "sleeve caught on something in Memphis." Apparently so. Or I wouldn't still be here, sitting around bored to death. So bored, in fact, that I have finally resorted to "the anus game," a profound time-passing game from my childhood, in which you substitute the word "anus" in movie titles. *Gone with the Anus. Remains of the Anus* (the Jeffrey Dahmer story). *The Anus of Miss Jane Pittman. Wuthering Anuses. The Anus of Oz. Twelve Angry Anuses* (the story of the Memphis City Council trying to agree on something). *An Anus to Remember*, and *The Nun's Anus*. There are the unforgettable classics — *Sorry, Wrong Anus; How Green Was My Anus, Three Anuses in a Fountain, Invasion of the Anus Snatchers*. There is the Bette Davis series — *Whatever Happened to Baby Anus; Hush, Hush, Sweet Anus*; and *A Pocketful of Anuses*. There's the much-loved Almodovar film *Woman on the Verge of a Nervous Anus*. And of course there are those holiday classics — *Anus on 34th Street, Anus in Connecticut, Yankee Doodle Anus*, and *It's a Wonderful Anus*. And now we will stop this, for it is apparent that I have finally sunk about as low as an adult who gets paid to write can possibly sink...

2

October 8–14, 1992

Sleeping with Florence Henderson

I was all set to write about the latest remarkable Dan Quayle remark: his whining that he's at a disadvantage in the election debates because he attended public schools while Al Gore was educated at private schools (if I'm not mistaken, "potato" is spelled the same way at both), and his suggestion that Rush Limbaugh moderate the presidential debates. And I was going to talk about Ross Perot having a campaign manager named Oscar Swindle, and about German housewife Ana Weiss, who recently sold one of her lungs to raise enough money to have her kitchen remodeled. But all that is old hat and none of it matters now, anyway. I'm too depressed to think about it. Unfortunately, while flipping through the paper the other day, my eyes landed on one of those "ten questions" tests designed to help the masses figure out if they fit into a certain category for which they need help. You know the kind: If you answer yes to at least half of these questions, then you're undoubtedly a guilt-ridden co-dependent substance abuser with an eating disorder. This particular test was laid out to help the reader decide whether he or she is depressed enough to warrant professional help. Call me a glutton for punishment, but I became transfixed on this test. And who wouldn't? First question: Do you feel downhearted, blue, and sad? Answer: Only when I wake up in the morning, reach over to the nightstand, and find that I'm out of cigarettes. Question No. 2: Do you not enjoy the things that you used to do? Well, I don't know, because obviously I don't do them anymore. Question No. 3: Do you feel that others would be better off if you were dead? Answer: Everyone except Commercial Credit, my mechanic, and the R.J. Reynolds Tobacco Company. Question No. 4: Do you feel that you are not useful or needed? Answer: Who cares? Question No. 5: Do you notice that you are losing weight? Answer: I wish. Question No. 6: Do you have trouble sleeping through the night? Answer: Yes, especially when I have those horrible nightmares about sleeping with Florence Henderson. Question

3

No. 7: Are you restless and can't keep still? Answer: I'm too busy pacing to think about it. Question No. 8: Is your mind not as clear as it used to be? Answer: I can't remember. Question No. 9: Do you get tired for no reason? Answer: I don't know, because all that pacing always provides a reason. Question No.10: Do you feel hopeless about the future? Answer: Oh, no. I can't wait to get old and lose my teeth and go blind and have to wear adult diapers and eat Alpo and find myself at the mercy of a bunch of sociopathic nursing-home attendants who are coping with their own frustrated lives by using me as a human pin-cushion. Thank god there were only ten questions. But that wasn't the end of it. Here's the little key they provided to help you decide if you're a bona-fide basket case. "If you answered 'yes' to at least five questions, and you answered 'yes' to question No. 1 or 2, and if these symptoms have persisted for at least two weeks you may be suffering from serious depression." Trying to figure that out is enough to depress anyone. The questionnaire also advises: "If you answered 'yes' to question No. 3 — regardless of how you answered the other questions — you should seek help immediately." In addition to this laundry list of things to ponder, there was an accompanying article that pointed out: A) Putting a plastic bag over your head frequently is not a good sign; B) There are medications that can help you want to go to the movies, and C) Electroshock therapy can still work wonders for certain people, although "some complain of memory loss, but that is usually fleeting." Boy do I feel better. Next time I feel down and out, I'll just grab the toaster and hop into the bathtub. And what's so bad about memory loss, anyway? If I could forget about half the things that happen every day, I might not even qualify for psychotherapy. All this got me to thinking about the validity of this and other similar tests, so I thought I'd give a shot at coming up with my own test — a much more simple and to-the-point list. Here goes: Question No.1: When you think of the possibility of George Bush getting re-elected, do you want to stick your head into a gas oven? 2: When you're not feeling quite up to par, does it not even help to watch *I Love Lucy* reruns? 3: Do you recoil in bone-chilling horror at the prospect of walking into a health spa or going to a public swimming pool? 4: Is your main reason for not committing suicide that no one else would know where your cat likes to be scratched? There, much simpler, huh? And I've even provided a much less complicated key: If you answered 'yes' to two or more of these questions, you might need help. If you answered 'yes' to question No. 1 and to question No. 3, will you go out with me? And that's that. Think about it, and decide for yourself just how nuts you really are...

July 1–7, 1993

Penis by the Slice

Concerned as I was over Burt and Loni's painful break-up, one other thing happened last week that makes anything else pale in comparison. In case you missed it in the news the other day, and I don't know how you could have, a woman in Manassas, Virginia, took a kitchen knife while her husband was asleep, and just whacked off his penis. True story. Chop, chop. Gone. Whacked it off. And that's not even the weird part. She then hopped in the car and fled the house, and as the story said, "unknowingly" took the penis with her. Unknowingly. I thought I'd heard everything, but how someone could leave the house with a cut-off penis and not know it is something I can't even begin to imagine. I mean, did she just grab it up with her keys and think it was part of her key chain? Did she throw it in her purse in a hurry? Did she stuff it accidentally into an eyeglass case thinking it was a pair of glasses? Just stuck it in her pocket without realizing it? I really want to understand this. And then, while stopped at a red light, she discovered she indeed had the penis in her possession. Can you imagine? Just looking down and saying to yourself, "Oh, look. It's my husband's chopped-off penis. How on earth did this get here?" And what did she do when she discovered she had the penis with her? Well, she just threw it out the car window into the street. Plunk! Like a half-eaten taco. Like the ring-toss at the fair, only it was the penis-toss. All of this was discovered when the husband woke up, realized his penis was missing, and somehow made it to the hospital. Now, don't you think he would have woken up during the middle of this? I crack an eye every time the cat meows; I certainly think I'd hop up from a deep sleep if someone was sawing away at my penis with a kitchen knife. Anyway, the hospital notified the police and they dispatched some officers to go to the couple's apartment in search of the missing penis, which they were unable to find. And can you imagine that scene? I mean, where do you start when you're looking for a chopped-off penis? But about that time, the woman called the police, told them that the husband had raped her and that she'd, er, cancelled his membership, then related the story of how she'd unknowingly (unknowingly; this is killing me) taken it with her and hurled it into the intersection. So they went and found it, packed it on ice like a cold beer, and took it to the hospital to sew it back on, in a procedure which I assume is called an addadicktome (also gives new meaning, from the wife's point of view anyway, to Stitchwitchery). As it turns out, they were able to sew the organ back on with nine-and-a-half hours of surgery, the wife was charged with aggravated malicious wounding, and no charges have been brought as of yet in the rape allegation. And get this: The article says the man is reported in "satisfactory condition." Wait a minute. He had his penis chopped off, it was thrown into the street, found, and re-attached, and he's feeling satisfactory?!!! I don't think so. What's he gonna do? Just go back home, act like nothing's wrong, pop in *Dick Tracy*, cook some hot dogs, and order her a set of Ginsu knives (cuts through anything!) for Christmas? If I were him, I'd take her straight to *People's Court*, and leave this in the hands of the wise Judge Wapner. I can hear him now: "Ma'am, did you indeed cut off your husband's penis? Sir, do you have the penis with you? Let me see it." You can imagine how the rest of that scenario would go. This is one *People's Court* I don't want to miss...

July 21–27, 1994

Death of a Shellfish

Can you believe it? Lobster Boy. Dead. Shot in the head and killed by a hit man hired by his own wife. A carnival freak slaying. Despite the fact that his deformity had rendered him wheelchair-bound, as the story has been reported, it seems that old Lobster Boy was still able to "pummel his wife and family with his two-fingered arms, head-butt them, and repeatedly threaten them with death," especially when he was all boozed up and wanted to take his frustrations out on those around him, leaving family members at the mercy of his clawlike hands. But you know, for some reason I don't buy this. Here his wife, Mary Stiles, was sitting in the courtroom sobbing as her attorney related the stories of how Lobster Boy, Grady Stiles, physically abused her until she simply had to have him killed. Well, I've got two questions for Mrs. Stiles: A) Precisely why did you marry someone named Lobster Boy in the first place? and B) When he got drunk and started trying to get rough, why didn't you do something simple, like, uh, walk away from him? It's not like he could really chase you around too fast. She even testified in court about one incident, in which she woke up to find a whiskey-breathed Lobster Boy holding a butcher knife to her throat threatening to kill her, but instead of letting her have it he simply "crawled away." Why didn't she do something then, like step on him? For God's sake, if the guy has to get around the house by crawling, how dangerous could he really be? If I'd been her, I would have simply fought back and tortured him with cruel remarks, like, "Get away from me, you little shrimp...oh, excuse me, I mean — ha, ha ha, aaaa ha ha ha ha ha! — you little lobster!" Or "Hit me one more time you lousy crustacean and your ass is out the thermadoor!" Or "No, I'm not having sex with you. I'm afraid you might give me crabs!" Or "What's the matter, Honey, constipated? Well, why don't you go pinch a loaf?!" She could also have done other fun things, like run him a boiling-hot bath and put lemon slices in it, or wrapped his clawlike hands with big rubber bands while he was sleeping. But, nay, she just stood around and took it. My favorite thing about this whole lobster tale (tee-hee) — aside from the fact that Mrs. Stiles actually married Lobster Boy not once but twice, with a divorce in between and a marriage to one Glenn Newman, known as "The World's Smallest Man." Not to mention the fact that Lobster Boy was shot while sitting in his underwear in their trailer in Florida (what were the odds?) — is this head-butting business. Correct me if I'm wrong, but wouldn't she have to have been standing there motionless right in front of him watching him rear his head back in order for him to be able to successfully butt her? Or could it have been that he just waited until she was off-guard, got going at a fast start, and zoomed across the room with his head bent down like a torpedo and rammed her in the gut? I'm really trying my best to get a mental picture of this. And what I'm getting is not pretty. I'm well aware that physical deformity and spousal abuse are not topics to be taken lightly, but really. This one kind of stands on its own from anything else. A carnival freak getting drunk and nasty and chasing his family around the house head-butting them and abusing them until they have to have him killed? Something tells me that maybe she just got sick and tired of being married to a carnival freak, even if she was stupid enough to leave The World's Smallest Man to remarry the Lobster Boy. God, how I would love to meet this woman. Can you imagine what kind of personal ad she would place in the paper? "Single white female seeking anyone who: 1) has a 14-inch tongue, 2) has two heads, 3) is actually a gorilla but has a human head, 4) is only a human head, severed long ago from its body but kept alive in a laboratory in South America, 5) is a body without a head at all, 6) bites the heads off of live chickens, and/or 7) has been rejoined to his Siamese twin by a cruel doctor because you didn't pay the bill after he parted you at birth with a butter knife." She'd probably end up with the same kind of dates I get. But that's another story for another time, or time capsule, I should say...

April 28–May 14, 1994

Lightin' Up

I am revolting. But not much more so than usual. I am revolting because I've heard just about as much about this non-smoking nonsense as I can stand to hear. It has finally made me crazier than I already was. I know that this issue of the *Flyer* has some coverage of the current anti-smoking frenzy, but at this writing I have no idea of what it's going to be. I assume it's going to be some sort of well-documented, balanced, objective, non-opinionated look into what's going on right now with the tobacco industry and the various medical institutions and so forth and so on and so on. But I am still revolting. Because I am one of those people who smoke, and I can tell you right now that chewing a piece of Wrigley's spearmint gum in non-smoking situations sucks the big one in the way of making me feel any better. In fact, I hate those people on that commercial. You know, the sickeningly chipper woman who says, "I am a smoker, but I ride in a car pool where no one else smokes. So I just pull out a stick of Wrigley's spearmint gum and enjoy the pure chewing satisfaction." Well, I can think of a few places to tell her to place that cud once she's finished with it. I am a smoker, and when I'm stuck in a situation where I can't smoke, the only thing that halfway appeases me is to gnaw on one of my limbs until I can get the hell somewhere else and light up. But I am a nice smoker. If I'm in the car or home or office of someone who's really bothered by cigarette smoke, I don't smoke, and I smile, and I act like it doesn't bother me. Which is why I feel I have the right to walk up and poke the eyes out of those people who cough and wave their arms and freak out when they're out in the middle of a field and someone lights a cigarette. Or even worse, when you're in a bar and some idiot starts raising hell over cigarette smoke. You want to just walk up to him, point out that he must have the I.Q. of a fence post, and give him the bulletin that he happens to be in a bar where people gather to smoke and stay away from the rest of the wretched world. Or just shoot him and be done with it. The most horrible part about all this non-smoking mania is that smoking is now forbidden in the very places where smokers absolutely must smoke to cope with the stress. Here, for example, is a true story: Just the other day, my pop had to have some pretty serious emergency surgery. I'm there in the middle of the night, worried to death, in the critical care waiting room, which is already like something out of a very surreal movie. And, of course, you're not allowed to smoke in the room. So, at about, oh, 2 o'clock in the morning, a woman appears and decides to strike up a conversation. She asks what I'm doing there. I tell her my dad is having surgery for an aneurism. Very flatly she replies, "Oh, that's what my husband's in for. His busted in the ambulance on the way down from Selmer. He was dead, right there in the ambulance, but they cut him open from top to bottom, and turned him over and dumped all his blood out and brought him right back to life. He's been in here eight days. Shoot, I had on the same clothes for the first four days. When I went to take off my socks, it wuz like they had just growed to my feet. But I finally got 'em peeled off and they was so stiff it looked like they still had feet in 'em! At least nobody came around and bothered me while I was a' trying to sleep. Sheeew-weee!" And somebody's trying to tell me that second-hand smoke is a health hazard. Please. Like I said, I'm revolting...

December 15–21, 1994

Nose Hairs Roasting on an Open Fire

Five o'clock in the morning. Sometime during the holiday season. I have just awakened from a nightmare. A few days ago, someone, unfortunately, mentioned to me that she, while Christmas shopping in one of our local malls, actually saw a woman walking through the little world o'retail wearing a pair of antlers on her head, apparently attached by some process that involves Velcro. When I went to sleep last night, I instantly began to writhe and roll about, on the couch, with visions of this woman dancing in my head. The *visions* were dancing, not her. She was following me. Not concerned with the details of exactly why this woman had chosen to come shopping at the mall dressed as livestock, I simply wanted to whip a .357 Magnum and place it directly between her eyes, but I was too scared of her to approach her. She was evil. She had demonic, Christmas-shopping eyes. And while all laws of the universe suggest that she was probably shopping for one of those varnished-plywood pen-and-pencil desk sets embellished with decoupaged images of Naomi and Wynonna Judd, I could only imagine her browsing through the housewares department, and suddenly snapping and going berserk, randomly trying to kill the other shoppers, as well as me, with a salad shooter. Naturally, I woke up screaming and gasping for breath, soon after which I smoked several cigarettes to calm my nerves and then proceeded to eat half of a leftover chocolate cake and consume massive quantities of coffee, although my hypoglycemic condition is severely endangered by any kind of sugar and/or coffee intake. But who cares? It makes me feel like Sunny Von Bulow, and it is, after all, such moments (not eating the cake and drinking the coffee, technically, but feeling like Sunny Von Bulow) that make life worth living, despite the fact that poor Sunny remains in a coma, "Brain dead, body better than ever," as the movie based on her life has her say in the narrative voice-over. Once I enjoyed the complete experience of identifying with Sunny, my thoughts again returned, however, to the woman-wearing-antlers nightmare, and the only way I could take my mind off of it was by reliving one of my most cherished holiday memories. A few years ago, I was with another equally angst-ridden friend on Christmas Eve, and for some reason we found ourselves driving around in the middle of the night in a small town adjacent to Memphis (I would say which town, but the city leaders there tend to be very sensitive and I don't need any more grief from them). We drove around in circles, lost, for a while, until finally we stopped into a convenience store that happened to be open after midnight. As we entered the store, we came face to face with the cashier, a woman wearing a Santa Claus hat and holding a mirror, all the while ripping the burly black hairs from her nose with a pair of tweezers and humming along with a Muzak rendition of "I saw Mommy Kissing Santa Claus," a song that to me, for some reason, has always suggested incest or some other decidedly left-of-center sexual behavior. The cashier removed the tweezers from her nose and stopped yanking out the nose hairs long enough to acknowledge us with a friendly, "Merry Christmas, fellers" but it was too late. I had already fled to the rear of the store and was doubled over with my head in the frozen food bin, tears running down my face, pretending to be shopping for peas and carrots. The scene was, from that moment, indelibly etched into my psyche, the only emotionally charged triumph of an otherwise terribly disturbing time of year, the only other redeeming quality of which is the fact that it stays damp, overcast, and gray much of the time, which I find intensely comforting, except for when the sun does occasionally peek out, startling me into an involuntary scare that it is the light you see at the end of a long corridor when you're dying. Or are in the beginning stages of fainting from a drop in blood sugar, something that always makes me feel somehow rejuvenated when I regain consciousness. I have even found recently that fainting and then coming to makes me alert enough to spot character actors in movies and recognize them from tiny bit parts they played in episodes of *I Love Lucy*. But I digress. We were talking about the woman wearing a pair of Velcro-attached faux antlers on her head. Moral of the story: If you have some type of psychological disorder that compels you to go shopping wearing this kind of accessory, please seek professional help immediately, or at least buffer the burden you place on those with whom you come into contact by plucking out nose hairs and shouting season's greetings. It makes things a lot easier on those of us whose desire for a lobotomy becomes even more heightened than usual during the holidays. And there you have it: another bright spot of Christmas cheer to help give you the spirit...

August 11–17, 1994

A Helluva Match

Yeah, yeah, yeah. Lisa Marie and Michael Jackson. Lisa Marie and Michael Jackson. Lisa Marie and Michael Jackson. That's all I've heard since it was confirmed that they did indeed sneak off to the Dominican Republic and were married. Well, I say, big fat deal. I don't know why everyone is so shocked and is sitting around trying to figure out why, oh, why, she has done this. Obviously, she has lived most of her life in California. Does this really need any further explanation? Apparently, it does to some, especially those dedicated Elvis fans who are about to go off the deep end because their King's little girl done gone and got herself hitched to some child-molestin' freak of nature whose plastic surgery bills make Phyllis Diller's look like the cost of a bag of Krystal chili-cheese puffs. And, love aside, I guess there is some reason to wonder about this odd union. Could it be that she married him for makeup secrets? She has, after all, been looking a little on the rough side on the tabloid covers, what with all that child-bearing and the ending of her first marriage. And we know that Michael has more experience with makeup than Dustin Hoffman had when filming *Tootsie*. Not that his is any work of art either, though. Or could it be that since Michael couldn't buy the skeleton of the Elephant Man he's settling for the Jungle Room and an airplane decorated in avocado green and harvest gold? Or does that jumpsuit collection simply bring back fond memories of his Jackson Five childhood? Who's to say? Some, of course, think the entire ordeal is merely a plot on the part of Lisa Marie's Scientology pals to recruit yet another powerful celebrity into their realm, claiming that that particular religion has a way of brainwashing people and milking their celebrity status for all its worth. Well, duh. Show me a religion that doesn't brainwash people and I'll eat my hat. You think those people who haul all the way to that monstrous-looking Bellevue Baptist Municipal Airport Church in the middle of nowhere every Sunday do it because they don't have anything better to do? Come to think of it, that's probably the case. Or did Michael marry her because she has a young son? He will, after all, be 11 years old someday. And there's the theory that this is just a huge business merger, giving Michael the rights now to not only the Beatles' music, but to the other greatest rock-and-roll entity ever. And if his late, great father-in-law left any medicine behind, this could also become the world's largest stash of Percodan. Whatever the case, you do have to wonder how this might affect Graceland. I certainly hope he's not planning to put an oxygen tent in the billiard room, thereby ruining the design of the 500 million bolts of pleated fabric. A few of his wild animals roaming the grounds wouldn't be a bad touch, but we already have that. Regardless, I think it's great. They're already off in Rumania handing out goodies to the war-torn children, so more power to them. Still, it will be interesting to find out the real story on this, which I'm sure will be the subject of a new book by Michael's hideous sister LaToya, who has probably already attempted to scratch Lisa Marie's eyes out for stealing yet more of the spotlight. But I guess we'll just have to wait and see...

May 26–June 1, 1994

A Brief Note to Jackie

I can't believe it. All of you people down there dressing up like pigs, eating that nasty barbecue and callin' hogs and rolling around drunk in the mud — while Jacqueline Bouvier Kennedy Onassis lay dead in her Manhattan apartment. Jackie, dead. The world lost the most wonderful woman it ever had, and you people were concerned only with who would be able to barbecue the best shoulder meat. Shame on you. When Nixon died a few weeks ago, the mail was stopped and the government practically shut down. For Nixon. But nooooo. When someone truly fabulous like Jackie O. dies, it's just business as usual. I am disgusted. Jackie is dead, the mail is still running, and I'm getting letters about men's underwear. That's right, men's underwear. And not just any underwear, mind you, but "Power Underwear." And I believe this company is serious. "The power tie in the workplace has long symbolized confidence, strength, and bravado," the Champion Products press kit states, but "men can now put aside their power tie and instead slip on a 'Power Liner,' available at department stores and sporting goods stores." Does this mean that instead of ties, men will now be wearing designer underwear around their necks? And more importantly, is this new underwear designed to stop that horrible "creeping" problem, which results in, as they say in the South, having a "goat in one's garden"? Regardless, this is very versatile underwear. "Whether running for a pass or hiking in the woods," the company goes on to say, "the Power Liner provides crucial, durable athletic support and protection. Men today are active participants in all areas of life, and require underwear that can keep up with their pace and lifestyle." Well, isn't that good to know? The company does not, however, point out the advantages of the Power Liner when men are doing what they normally do — sitting around drinking beer, picking their noses, scratching their butts, and watching female American Gladiators duke it

15

out on television. And here's a revelation from the friendly underwear folks at Champion Products: "Something exciting is happening underneath men's clothing these days." Are they talking about Pee Wee Herman? John Bobbitt's miracle surgery? No. They're talking about the average Joe. "Increasingly," they point out, "men are choosing different underwear for different occasions." Boy, that's me, all right. Just this morning I was planning what sort of fashion statement to make when I was getting ready to go to Piggly Wiggly, and that pesky problem of what style of underwear to put on came up. Let's see, should it be basic white briefs or colorful boxers? A breezy tank top, or a short-length Lycra support liner? It used to be so simple, before I found out that the underwear I wear is reflective of my personal taste and lifestyle choices, not to mention the fact that Champion tells me I'm a "busy man who demands day-long comfort in my athletic and leisure activities." Yes, I indeed do like to feel that I'll be not only comfortable but stylish as well as I'm partaking of my favorite athletic and leisure activities — trying to ascertain whether or not to refill the radiator and put oil in my car before heading out to the video store to rent several bad movies and to stop, of course, and pick up a carton of cigarettes and cat food, thereby giving me plenty to keep me occupied for the weekend and good reason not to answer the telephone or the door under any circumstances whatsoever. I usually don't talk about my underwear in public, but I did end up choosing the basic white briefs — the clean pair, the one with only one or two small holes, the one I had to get my cat off of to pull them out of the pile of laundry that's been sitting on the bed for a week. So I guess that means, in short (or in shorts, as it were), that underneath my clothes there is nothing exciting going on. Go figure. And anyway, who cares? Jackie's dead. Which is why I couldn't care less about what's going on around town this week (well, that and the fact that I never care), but since I get paid to write this drivel, I guess I'd better do it — even though I'd much rather be in Atlantic City covering the controversial case in which Dom DeLuise has been accused of touching a 24-year-old male casino employee in a sexual way. Can you imagine ? But I'm not there covering that; I'm here, stuck doing this. And Jackie's dead...

July 7–13, 1994

Ain't Too Proud To Beg

This column is for Percy Ross, and I fully intend to send it to him. Ross, as you probably know, is the millionaire who hands out money via his syndicated Q&A newspaper column, in which people write to him asking for money and he responds with a yeah or nay and decides whether or not to hand over some loot. The last one I read included a letter from some kid whining about not having enough clothes and about her mother having to wear sweatpants to work. And Ross, obviously a pushover or a man with political aspirations, gave the brat some money. What's so odd about wearing sweatpants to work? Hasn't Ross ever been to Parkway Village? Everyone there does it and you don't see them whimpering about it. So, Mr. Ross, here are the reasons why I think you should give me several million dollars. I have plenty of clothes, but unfortunately I can't wear most of them because gravity and time have not been especially kind. I've been on a diet since I was eight years old, and now, at almost 35, the old· spare tire just won't go away. I guess I could consider exercising, but who wants to waste time with that kind of crap, and besides, the thought of jumping around doing high kicks in a room full of people dressed in spandex makes me violently ill. So could you please foot the bill for me to have liposuction? Not a lot. Just enough so that I will no longer shriek when forced to walk past a full-length mirror. I also need money for extensive travel. As I'm writing this, it happens to be July 4th, and it's making me very depressed to think that I live in a country where the entire populace is gripped with the tension over what is in an envelope involved in the O.J. You-Know-Who trial. Not to mention the controversy about how many hairs he had to give the investigators. (It's a good thing they've never asked me to hand over 100 hairs; they'd be hard-pressed to find 20 on this cue-ball). I also live in a country where Dan Quayle comes to my own home town to sign copies of his new book and people actually show up to see him, where the easiest way to make some quick money is to beat up on your wife so much that she finally whacks off your penis and you sell your story to all of the TV stations and tabloids and then go on the comedy club circuit as a professional comedian, where people like Ross Perot are allowed to appear on television, and where people like Rush Limbaugh are allowed to live. I tell you, Percy, it's all too depressing, and I need to beat a path to another continent. I think if you'd send me enough money to shack up in a Swiss chateau for a few years, I might feel a little better. And if I should ever return to the good old U.S. of A., I'm going to need quite a bit of money, because I'm going to build my own city. A city in which it is illegal not to smoke. No smokeless buildings, no nonsmoking sections in restaurants, and no obnoxious "No Smoking" signs on buses and in public restrooms. In fact, cigarettes, in this city, will be free. I'll give them out like the government gives out free cheese. And when someone walks in and sits down at a table in a bar or restaurant and does not immediately light a cigarette, the person next to him or her will lean over with a look of disgust and say, "Excuse me, but your not smoking is really bothering me, so would you please either light up or get out?" The only nonsmoker allowed in the town would be Hillary Clinton, because her anti-smoking policy is her only flaw, as far as I can tell, and I think we can convert her, thereby making her absolutely perfect. It would be such a lovely place, Percy, if only I had the money to build it. Also, if you would send me some money, I'd never have to work again, which means I wouldn't have to write this schlock every week of my life. Forget that goofy little girl and her despondency over her mother wearing sweatpants to work and give some of that money to a much more worthy cause: me. There. I'm going to send this off to Mr. Ross tomorrow, and we'll see what happens...

July 14–20, 1994

The Drag Queen Made Me Do It

This is never going to be over. Never. They've finally decided to try O.J. Simpson for murder, and you can bet we'll have to hear about his every breath until that happens. In the meantime, the *Globe* has finally shed some real light on the state of things, with its current cover story, "O.J.'s DAD WAS DRAG QUEEN WHO DIED OF AIDS!" Their take is that O.J. turned out to be such a brute because of the embarrassment he suffered during childhood over the fact that his father liked to dress up in women's clothing. (It's a good thing he didn't already have his nickname then; can you imagine the fruit juice jokes?). I hope they're not going to say this was one of those cases of "recovered memory." Something we all know is highly suspect. What, O.J. was hanging around the house one night, and suddenly he recalled that his father was a cross-dresser and the first thing that occurred to him was to go over and chop up his ex-wife and her boyfriend? Please. This is not nearly as believable as a quote from yet another tabloid, which stated that Jacqueline Kennedy Onassis left behind diaries, the contents of which are now being leaked, and include the passage: "Lady Bird's Texas ways drive me crazy. She's purely hick. Every time she tries to tell me something about running the White House I want to strangle her!" Anyone could believe that. And who could blame her? But O.J. committing a heinous double-murder just because he suddenly remembered seeing his father sashaying around the house in a cocktail dress, and according to a family friend, "a light-brown wig that was curly on top and had bangs combed forward"? C'mon. And who really cares? I know, I know, the whole country does, but that doesn't come as any real shocker. And don't think for a minute that writing about it isn't about to make me toss my lunch; it's just that there's nothing else in the collective American psyche right now that merits much of a mention. There is that doctor in Knoxville who was recently shot in his office when he pulled a loaded gun on some cops; it was later learned that he had in his possession numerous photographs of several naked Knoxville police officers. But I doubt that that trial will be aired on live television. Too bad. You can bet there's as much juice to that as there is to O.J. Maybe one day this ridiculous trial will finally be over and we can return to normal. Once again, if you ask me, the entire matter should be handled on *People's Court*. We all know that Judge Wapner would never let this get so dragged out. After all, he has to settle his cases in 15 minutes. And you can bet that he wouldn't put up with any whining about whether or not the evidence should be admissible in court or anything like that. If he saw that envelope with the mystery object in it, he'd do the smart thing and have Rusty the bailiff rip it open and let everyone see what was in it. And after the trial, O.J. would get to comment on the verdict on the way out in a brief but important discussion with Doug Lewellen. Yep, Judge Wapner has a way of taking the bull by the horns and getting things handled quickly. In fact, he should have taken over the whole Michael Jackson affair. Wapner: "Is there something distinguishing about your penis, Mr. Jackson, as little Danny has said, or is there not?" Jackson: "Well, your honor, I really don't think..." Wapner: "I don't care what you think. You whip that thing out now and we'll just see for ourselves." That would have been justice. Not that I'd really want to see Michael Jackson's penis on television or anywhere else, but at least it would have hurried things along. Which you can bet would happen if this whole O.J. thing was turned over to the Judge. Wapner: "Mr. Simpson, why did you kill your ex-wife?" Simpson: "Well, your honor, you see, I suddenly remembered that my father sometimes wore women's clothing, and I kind of went nuts." Wapner: "Excuse me, Mr. Simpson, but I don't care if your father stood in the middle of Central Park in a taffeta ball gown belting out old Barbra Streisand songs. That's no excuse for killing anyone." And there, with a smack of the gavel, it would finally all be over. But then, I'm sure another O.J. or Tonya Harding or Michael Jackson or Shannen Doherty or something will come along, so that we can show the rest of the world how asinine we really are...

April 7–13, 1994

The Hog Pen

A nice relaxing day in the country. Right. I don't know why I do this once or twice a year, but I get this bright idea that I need to get away from all the stress and strain of the daily grind and go out into the wilds, where there are no fax machines or traffic or neighbors, like the ones who live in my neighborhood, who not only seem to be worshipping the devil, but at the same time blare the song "We're So Sorry, Uncle Albert" at top volume from an eight-track stereo system. So when some people invited me to spend some time in the country the other day, I took them up on it. I had, after all, just undergone the trauma of making the mistake of looking into one of those three-way full-length mirrors at a department store, which had rendered me a quivering freak. So away we went. First of all, this place in the country happened to be in Arkansas, and when you enter Arkansas, there's a big sign announcing that this is the home state of President Bill Clinton. Well, that alone is enough to piss one off, because it immediately brings to mind the current Republican witch-hunt of which Bill and Hillary are the target for some mystical wrongdoing that may or may not have happened. And let's just cut straight to the chase with Hillary: If some man had taken $1,000 and turned it into $100,000, you can bet he'd be hailed as a financial genius. But nooo, it makes Hillary a mean old greedy thief. And why does everyone think she must have done something unethical to make that kind of return on her investment? Here's a bulletin: Could it be that she is smart? It's not like she wasn't in a state where 90 percent of the population has to be trained with wheelbarrows as children to learn to walk on just their hind legs. How stiff could the investment- market competition have been? But back to this trip. Going to Arkansas from Memphis, of course, requires driving through the metropolis of West Memphis, and I'm sorry, but there are just no redeeming qualities about this town. One of the first things I saw was some sort of mini-amusement

park/recreation facility for children with lots of awful-looking outdoor
things to climb on, etc. The name of this roadside place to play: The Hog
Pen. Nice, huh? A week ago I was walking down the lovely palm-lined
Esplanade Boulevard in New Orleans and now I'm driving past The Hog
Pen in a state whose roster of cities includes one called Bald Knob. And
then there are the various gathering spots for truckers, at one of which
you can take a shower and buy peaches all at once. Somehow, this seems
rather creepy. Naked truckers and peaches. I don't trust it one bit. How
did Hillary live in this state as long as she did? And let us not neglect to
mention the interstate system in West Memphis, which was apparently
designed by the same person who invented the Mouse Trap board game. At
one point, we were driving in a lane facing oncoming traffic, and it was
supposed to be that way. But we made it out alive. And then it was on to
the country for a smaller highway. On this scenic route, we passed another
sort of outdoor playground, which featured a swing set and a jungle gym
and a merry-go-round and a fountain. It was right in the middle of a
cemetery. I guess the kiddies are supposed to play here while some one a
few feet away is being laid to rest, their spirit looking forward to an
eternity of plastic flowers and folded, praying hands. We passed several
other interesting places that offer a variety of services and "live minners,"
and we finally to the destination: a very nice, rustic, wonderful house on a
lake. Peaceful. Beautiful. Nature at its finest. Until, that is, you try to sleep.
Being the avid outdoorsman that I am, I decided to try to sleep outside,
albeit on a screened porch. First of all, the lovely weather gave way to a
crashing thunderstorm at, oh, about 3 o'clock in the morning and the
temperature dropped, oh, about 25 degrees. At least, I thought to myself,
this will drive the snakes I'm having nightmares about back into wherever
it is they stay when they're not out slithering around trying to kill people.
So I finally go back to sleep, once the thunder stops. Then the sun begins
to come up. Which means that every bird within a five-mile radius wakes
up at the same time and starts to make its own little sound. Some screech.
Some whistle. Some make sounds that resemble the ones my neighbors
make when they are singing along with "We're So Sorry, Uncle Albert"
while worshipping the devil. And right outside the porch where I'm trying
to sleep is a woodpecker, which might as well be a concrete drill at this
point. It is barely daylight, I'm in the middle of nowhere, and I've never
heard so much racket in my life. By this point, my nerves are shot to hell.
I'd like to fax a rescue note to someone in civilization, but there's no
machine. Nor is there a video store or a Williams-Sonoma outlet store or a

food market where the main staple isn't rag bologna and "live minners." Nor is there even a television, which I really wanted to watch, because on *Talk Soup* Greg Kinnear was scheduled to show a clip of *The Montel Williams Show* that featured someone who'd been suspended from high school 12 times for having hair that was "too high." But it was okay, because I knew I'd be leaving soon, and I'd get to go back through West Memphis. Sometimes seeing the old Memphis skyline isn't so bad...

February 24–March 2, 1994

Danglin' in the Wind

Forget about Tonya Harding, health-care reform, and Anfernee's new movie. There's a man running up and down Summer Avenue totally naked except for a gold lamé vest, and he's carrying a purse and a pair of shoes in his hand! Or at least he was running up and down Summer Avenue Friday morning. Apparently during rush-hour traffic. Coincidentally, this happened to be the morning after the *Flyer's* gala fifth anniversary party, but no, we don't think the man was a member of the *Flyer* staff, although several employees were definite suspects until they showed up at work fully clothed. So far, the identity of the man in the vest is unknown; naturally, *The Commercial Appeal* didn't print a word about this story. They wasted all that space in Sunday's paper talking about Mayor W.W. Herenton's vision for the city of Memphis (har, har), and there hasn't even been a mention about the lamé-clad naked man with a purse and stilettos in his hands. So not only do we not know who this man is, but we also don't have any idea exactly why he was running up and down Summer Avenue, completely naked except for a gold lamé vest. I suppose the answer, my friends, was danglin' in the wind. Perhaps he was on his way to Stein Mart? Or on his way *from* Stein Mart? Maybe this was some sort of demonstration in an effort to have the name changed to Donna Summer Avenue. Surely, he couldn't have been leaving Sweet's 4-Wheel Drive Trailer Hitch and Lounge, although that notion is not without a certain degree of appeal. Whatever the case, there's nothing I like more than a naked drag queen running up and down the street. Though I think if I were going to be arrested for such a crime, I would at least choose a more acceptable avenue. After all, on Summer Avenue, who's really going to pay any attention? More than likely, it was the ice storm that provoked this behavior; it just seems to have driven people to the brink. Just look at how Ice Storm '94 is affecting people in Mississippi. Hell, Janet Reno has had to call in the troops to the tiny and once-quiet town of Ovett, because the townsfolk have been harassing a group of lesbians who've established a commune on a pig farm! I wonder how the fine people of Ovett would feel if they had naked men in gold lamé vests running up and down the streets of their little Baptist hamlet. And back here in Memphis, one day during the storm I was fortunate enough to see a man unzip his fly, pull out the old Johnson (in that cold), and urinate in the middle of the street on which the *Flyer* offices are located. Isn't that pleasant? Perhaps he was a disgruntled reader. This was as I was leaving for lunch. I did not order Kielbasa. I did, however, dine at my favorite Asian restaurant, Saigon Le, where my fortune cookie suggested the following: "Laugh and the world laughs with you, snore and you sleep alone." Didn't say a word about urinating in the street. This is the same restaurant at which, during a recent Vietnamese New Year party when the city was still on ice, I was corralled into my first karaoke experience, and found myself in front of a sizeable crowd of people singing "Play That Funky Music, White Boy," followed by a beautiful rendition of "Love Grows Where My Rosemary Grows." Unfortunately, this has been captured on videotape, and I do not have the financial means to make blackmail payments. And speaking of video, once the power came back on at my house, I found myself watching the MTV Top 10 Video Countdown, and finally saw the massively popular Snoop Doggy Dog, whose video came in at Number Two. I would much rather have seen the naked man in the gold lamé vest on Summer Avenue. The main thing that bothered me was that I couldn't figure out what's up with this Snoop Doggy Dog. Is this some form of raw talent that I simply don't have the faculties to comprehend? And why has this man chosen that unfortunate — and not altogether un-Buckwheat-like — hairstyle which makes him look as if he slept with a cantaloupe attached to the top of his head? I mean, it's not as though it's some birth defect that can't be corrected. And he is selling enough records to bring in professional help. This hair is much more prone to damage the minds of our American youth than any lyrics he might spout. They should put a warning label on his albums that says "Caution: This man got some nappy hair." It's a good thing Snoop Doggy wasn't here for Ice Storm '94, because if that hair had iced over his head would've snapped off. Ah, but we can only dream, as we pull together as a people and try to put back together the pieces of our lives. And speaking of which, now that Ice Storm '94 is all but a chilling memory (except, of course, to those who still don't have power and are now gnawing off their own limbs), it's time to get back out and run naked through the streets...

July 28–August 3, 1994

Campaign in the Ass

A special issue dedicated to local politics. I would write about that this week to keep things streamlined, but I find the topic so staggeringly boring that I'm afraid I'd fall asleep at the keyboard. I haven't had any interest in local politics, in fact, since city councilman Jimmy Moore was found selling condoms in a public square in Moscow, or since councilman Ricky Peete was caught taking payola at a Shoney's restaurant (how gauche; not taking the money illegally, but taking it at a Shoney's, of all godforsaken places). Let's just face it: Until Memphis gets a woman mayor, it will always be good old boys against blacks, and that's just the way it is. Period. Much more so than Democrats vs. Republicans, conservatives vs. liberals. And while we're at it, let's just face one more thing: There ain't a rocket scientist in the bunch. Of course, anyone smart enough to be a rocket scientist would have the good sense not to become involved in Memphis politics, so you can't really fault the collective wisdom of the powers that be. Come to think of it, when you look at the local constituency, the politicos aren't so far down there on the chain of evolution. I guess as long as no one in power proposes a tax increase on Skoal, Budweiser, or gypsy-shag haircuts, nobody's feathers are going to get all that ruffled. I can say all this, because I, yes I, have been in politics in the past. I vividly recall that hotly debated race way back when, when I ran against a cheerleader in high school for the esteemed office of student council president, or something. Whatever it was, it was a big race. Campaign posters. Hand-outs. Speeches. Buying votes. Making promises I had no intention whatsoever of fulfilling. Spreading ugly rumors about that vile slut…er, my wonderful opponent. Just like real politics. Naturally, this was all done

26

from the "smoke hole," the designated area where all of the civilized people gathered to smoke cigarettes before and after and in-between classes — when we decided to attend class, which, believe me, wasn't on a daily basis. And needless to say, I represented a certain sect of the student population who needed strong leadership: those who had a hard time distinguishing reality from hallucinations. In fact, if I'm not mistaken, I probably came up with my campaign strategy while skipping school and sitting at Zinnie's. The strategy: Forget the stupid campaign and sit at Zinnie's. It worked for me. See, and all you high-school kids out there reading this should take note: When you do something like run for president of the student council, you can get away with murder. It doesn't matter how much of a deadbeat you are; it looks like you're a dedicated, responsible student, and the faculty sees you in a new light. And they'll excuse just about anything. "Tim, we see that you haven't been to school in four days and you have no sick note from your parents." "Well, Mrs. Ugly-old-haint-of-a-history-teacher, that's because I've been hard at work trying to come up with ideas that will enhance the relationship between student and teacher, thereby increasing the quality of life on campus for everyone involved." "Oh, well, then, that's fine. Just fine. You keep up the good work." Or: "Tim, you seem a little strange today and you smell a little funny and your eyes are bloodshot. What's going on?" "Well, you see, Mr. Idiot-football-coach-who-someone-had-the-poor-judgment-to-designate-as-a-math-teacher, I've been out in the parking lot trying to save some of our school's poor, lost souls who smoke that evil marijuana before class." "Oh, well, then, that's quite all right. You keep this up and one day you'll be president." And while I never became president — hell, I lost the high-school election to the cheerleader — I did learn some valuable lessons about the ways of politics: Lie and cheat, and you'll come out on top. However, I never found out what happened to the cheerleader. Since I don't have enough active brain cells left to remember her name, and since the idea of attending a class reunion is beneath discussion, I guess I'll never know. Unless she makes herself known. So if you were a cheerleader at beautiful Wooddale High School and ran for the student council presidency in 1977, please write the *Flyer* and let us know whatever happened to you. We hope you managed to avoid women's prison and the nickname Ice-Pick Mama. One last note: For those of you who are interested in local politics and are trying to decide for whom to vote for county mayor, let me just share this campaign promise from the candidate of candidates, Robert "Prince Mongo" Hodges: "Mongo will drastically reduce crime by invoking the caning law for people who commit minor crimes. Those who commit heinous crimes such as rape, dope dealers, robbers, and murderers will be executed before a firing squad. I will demand a speedy trial for all criminals. They will be tried and sentenced within 33 minutes of said crime." There. If only he'd been around to counsel me when I was running for that high-school office. But he wasn't and that was 200 years ago and who the hell really cares...

February 2–8 1995

Clip, Clop, Bang!

Man, am I ever bored. Really bored. So bored I'm tempted to again play the anus game (that oh-so-popular pastime I mentioned a few weeks ago in which you replace words with the word "anus" in the titles of songs, movies, and plays, like *Ain't No Anus High Enough, Anus Too Short to Box with God* and *On Top of Old Anus*). But I won't stoop to that again. Although, I did see a fun use of verbiage the other day in a newspaper from another city, which kind of thrilled me in a similar manner; it was an ad for a porno movie titled *Foreskin Gump*. The only other thing I've seen this week that came close to working me up that much was one of the new bad furniture commercials, in which a woman is running around the store saying she'll take this and she'll take that. All the while followed by a black man carrying a clipboard and writing down what she wants, and occasionally looking into the camera and rolling his eyes, as if to say, "Who is this crazy cracker?!" It's positively destined for cult status. And here in the very civilized neighborhood I live in now, with its drought of idiosyncrasies, I did see in the wee hours of the morning the other day a man walking his dog down the sidewalk, dressed in normal attire save for the hat atop his head that was made to look like a head of lettuce. Thank God I never sleep. Anyway, like I said, I am really bored and have nothing to say. So I've decided to simply make this week's column a list of my favorite jokes — bad ones, stupid ones, and best of all, some very politically incorrect, offensive, tasteless ones, which, of course, are my favorites. Here goes: What is it when you hear Clip, clop, bang! Clip, clop, bang!? An Amish drive-by shooting. A horse walks into a bar. The bartender says, "Hey, why the long face?" What time is it when it's time to go to the Chinese dentist? Two thirty. A Japanese girl gets up at her school assembly to make a speech wearing very thick glasses, and the principal says, "What's wrong? Do you have a cataract?" "No," she says. "My family drives a Lincoln." Woman goes to the doctor, and he tells her that although it sounds very strange, he guarantees she will lose weight if instead of eating her food she places it into her rectum. She goes back to see him several weeks later for a checkup, and she is frantically shifting her weight from one leg to the other, moving her hips from side to side. "What's wrong?" the doctor asks in a very concerned voice. "Are you having some side effects from the new diet?" "Oh, no," she replies nonchalantly. "I'm just chewing gum." A man walks into a psychiatrist's office and says. "Doctor, you gotta help me. I'm a nervous wreck. I feel like a tepee and a wigwam!" "Relax," the doctor says, "You're just two tents." A German man, a Mexican man, and an Asian man go to work in a warehouse. German man is in charge of shipping, Mexican man is in charge of the dock, Asian man is in charge of supplies. The supervisor goes to check on them. German man has everything under control and Mexican man is hard at work on the dock, but the Asian man is nowhere to be found. Supervisor walks through the warehouse looking for him, and the Asian man jumps out from behind a corner and screams, "Supplies!" If two heterosexual salesmen and two gay male salesmen from a candy company were going on a trip to a convention, who would get there first? Why, the straight people, of course, because the two gay guys would still be at home packing their shit. What's foreplay in Frayser? "Get in the truck, bitch!" Little Jimmy stands up in class to tell a story for show-and-tell. "Yesterday," he says, "I saw a Chihuahua chasing a German shepherd, and when the German shepherd finally ran into a fence, the Chihuahua went right up his butthole!" "Jimmy!" the teacher admonishes. "That's rectum." "Rectum, hell," Jimmy says. "It killed 'em!" And that one just about killed me, especially when I heard it 20 years ago...

May 19–25, 1994

Bette and Joan

This might be my last column. That is if someone out there doesn't somehow get me a videotape of *Tears and Laughter: The Joan and Melissa Rivers Story*. I am positively sick that I missed this made-for-television slice of Americana, and I'm sure that it was a masterpiece. I can only pray that the script includes the scene which Joan has sworn is true — when she and Melissa showed up for Edgar's memorial service and were not allowed in because it had already started and some strange rule prevented those in charge from letting in even the grieving widow and daughter, at which point Joan simply turned on her heel to Melissa and said, "C'mon. Let's go shopping." Naturally, no matter how wonderful the rocky story of Joan and Melissa is, it couldn't possibly hold a candle to the all-time best mother-and-daughter-relationship-on-the-skids film, *Mommie Dearest*, the ultimate classic which chronicles the lives, of course, of Joan and Christina Crawford. Now that I've seen it maybe 20 times or more, I've decided that my favorite scene is when Joan tries to make a very young Christina eat a slab of rare meat. Christina whines, "But Mommie, blood runs all out of it when I push on it." To which Joan (played by Faye Dunaway in arguably her finest hour) replies with a growl, "Then don't push on it!" Nothing short of sheer filmmaking brilliance. That, and the fact that Faye Dunaway's makeup — a character in itself— looks more natural in the scene in which she's laid out dead in a coffin than at any other time in the movie. And need I even mention the emotional surge I feel during the scene in which Mommie bludgeons little Christina with a Dutch Cleanser can — on the very night that she won her Oscar? You'd think that Joan would have been in a halfway decent mood. Come to think of it, maybe she was. I could go on and on for hours about this lovely movie, but I'm afraid it will only make me stop working and rush out to rent it — just one more time. And while no mother-daughter film could ever reach the pinnacle of pleasure that *Mommie Dearest* provides, it was indeed wise of Joan and Melissa to film their story now, while all the other good TV movies are still in the making and won't be out until who knows when. What about poor Michael Fay, the youth who was recently caned in Singapore? And who, in case you haven't heard, has already been arrested again — for smoking crack. I'm sure that a movie will be made about this, if not for no other reason then that the American public is dying to see the caning, or at least a realistic re-enactment of it. Maybe the new Tonya Harding story could be scripted so that she, too, gets caned — not for having her ex-husband attack Nancy Kerrigan, but for, of course, her choice of hairstyle. And now that Bette Davis has kicked the bucket, why hasn't someone made a movie about the relationship between her and her daughter B.D. Hyman? If you haven't read Joe Queenan's review of Bette's and B.D.'s autobiographies in this month's issue of *Movieline* magazine, I suggest that you rush out and buy it instantly. Queenan points out that in B.D.'s viscious book about her mother (which was published while Bette was still alive, right after she'd had a mastectomy), she accuses Bette of having been "a slut, a drunk, a child abuser, a liar, a pig, and a woman known to appear at the top of the stairs during a party in a see-through nightie and tell the assembled throng below that she would like a glass of warm milk." Not only that, but B.D. says that Bette's fourth husband, Gary Merrill, "used to stroll around the house sipping martinis stark naked when she was a little kid, scaring the hell out of the maids." Why has this not been adapted for film? I think someone should do it immediately, . using, of course, an all-male cast of female impersonators. And it should include at least a few re-enacted scenes from Bette's movies, in particular the historic scene from *Hush, Hush, Sweet Charlotte*, when Bette has invited Olivia de Havilland to come help her save the plantation, and finds out that de Havilland, "Cuzin Miriam," has no intention of doing so, at which point Bette rises from her chair at the dinner table and screams, "You vile, sorry bitch! What did you think I asked you here for, company?!" It could be one swell piece of film, eh? Maybe before the movie is made, I'll pen a stage version, and take it on the road, presenting it at mental institutions and rehab centers as entertainment therapy. After, of course, a tour of elementary schools and day-care centers...

March 24–30, 1994

One Bulbous Butt

Just in case you were worrying, here's a bit of good news, in the way of a newspaper headline: "The bigger your butt, the smarter you are!" This, according to Chicago psychologist Dr. Milton Sternes, whose five-year buttocks study will be chronicled in his upcoming book, *Big Butt, Bigger Brains*, to be released some time this spring. And no, this is not one of those revolting self-help books that takes you through the steps to get in touch with your feelings about your big butt and then learn to talk to yourself in the mirror about it via a morning affirmation session. It's just the straight facts about big butts and high I.Q.s. But even more important than this, the same issue of this particular newspaper has provided a list of guidelines on the one thing that plagues people every day: how to meet new people. I guess if you have a big butt, you're probably smart enough to do this on your own, but if not, here are some of the "surefire" tips on how to make new friends from Tulane University professor Dr. Frederick Koenig: 1) "Notice things about people and comment on them! Give them your impression of their jewelry, hairdo, shirt, or tie. Most people love this kind of attention." Of course, Koenig failed to point out other comments that can help, such as, "Gee, madam, you certainly have one bulbous butt; you must be quite intelligent." Or, "My, that is an interesting hairdo. Exactly what color is that?" It's one I've never seen in nature." Do not, however, make the mistake of telling a bald person he has a "nicely shaped head." Several people have said this to me, and I have written their names on a list for future use, and it's not going to be pretty. As for jewelry, I've always found that this one works: "Wow, that necklace looks great on you. You are so lucky to be able to wear cheap dime-store costume jewelry and get away with it." 2) Koenig suggests that you "carry something with you that will spark conversation. Carry a book with an unusual title or carry an unusual magazine; these items are sure conversation starters." Well, first of all, when it comes out, I'd definitely recommend *Big Butt, Bigger Brains*. I, personally, have tried this with my copy of *Milwaukee Massacre: The Shocking Story of America's Most Twisted Sex Killer*, and you know, it was odd; no one in the gourmet food store where I was shopping acted like they wanted to meet me. Go figure. And just look at all the friends Damien Echols made at school by carrying around a dog skull. And, once again, I offer as proof of this particular theory the story about a dear friend of mine who, at a certain "difficult" time in his life, carried with him everywhere he went a bowling ball he affectionately referred to as Darlene. Darlene went with us to parties, to restaurants, on out-of-town trips (she was actually kidnapped at one point and was forced into a life of prostitution in Oklahoma until the ransom was paid. Can you imagine? Having to be a prostitute in Oklahoma? How less-than-chic). And Darlene certainly helped my friend meet people. Most of them looked as if they had perhaps undergone some horrible psychological trauma during childhood that rendered them unable to form a complete sentence, but they were nice just the same. Except for that one person who placed Darlene in the toilet at a party and urinated on her. Poor thing. She was a fun bowling ball, but just not into water sports. Back to Dr. Koenig. He also suggests that you "advertise for a friend in the paper." Wrong. I did this once as a joke and ended up almost having my eyes pecked out by a parakeet at a house in Bartlett that was decorated in a country-craft motif. I have had more pleasant experiences. Like the time I was having dinner with someone who, unbeknownst to me at the time, was a mortician, and his beeper went off, signaling the fact that he had to leave to go pick up a dead body. What luck. No, no offense to the wonderful *Flyer* personals, but you can keep your newspaper advertisements. Dr. Koenig goes on to recommend several other surefire ways to meet new people, but let's dispense with that now and address a much more important issue: how to avoid meeting new people at all costs, which makes much more sense to me...

March 4–10, 1993

Them Tattoos

Well, I hope you're all happy now that you've almost given Harold Ford a heart attack. Maybe it's just me, but I don't understand what the big fat deal is. What did he allegedly do? Sort of borrow some money from some big bank and sort of get out of paying it back? Well, pardon me for livin', but what's so shocking about that? I guess it's all right for ex-prez George Bush to have his little weenies illegally spy on Bill Clinton and his mother during the election and get away with it. I guess it's all right that he was selling arms to Middle-Eastern countries right and left and filtering the loot to contras who used it to ravage their own countries and kill thousands of innocent people. I guess it's all right that his son Neil swiped about a billion dollars during the S&L scandal and walked away scot-free. I guess it was all right for former first lady Nancy Reagan to borrow all those hideous $25,000 dresses from famous designers and never return them or pay for them. But let one powerful black congressman — who, let it be noted here, has an impeccable voting record — get into a little trouble and, BAM!, he's all but lynched. Eleven white jurors and one black, shipped in from a county that, if it's possible, has an even higher redneck population than this one? Oh, yeah, that sounds like a real fair trial to me. I can hear the deliberations now: "Well, Bubba, whadduya thank?" "Shoot, Lester, I don't know. I say we just go ahead and say he's guilty, or else we're gonna be stuck here all day and miss the tractor pull tonight. Besides, I'm tired. Me and my old lady got into it last night and I had to stay up all night to make sure she didn't call up and charge nothin' on the shoppin' channel." "Lerlen, do you thank he's guilty?" "Oh, I don't know, Betty Lou, I ain't really paid that much attention, 'cause I couldn't really keep up with what them lawyers were talkin' about. Did you see Cher on *Oprah* the other day? I just can't believe she's 47 and was on there talkin' about her 25-year-old boyfriend. And I don't think she's one bit ashamed about them tattoos she has all over her body. I couldn't never do that. My Uncle Tommy did, though. He had a tattoo of a beagle chasing a rabbit right up his butt. I thank he did it so his wife would leave him, but she said it didn't bother her one bit 'cause she wasn't gonna be looking back there anyway. That Cher don't look bad though, if she'd have her a nose job, she'd be right pretty." "Yeah, she would. I just loved her in *Moonstruck*, when she played that Italian girl. You know, I hope we're not supposed to be writin' down our verdicts on those little scraps of paper, 'cause I had to use mine a while ago to get a piece of Vienna sausage out of my teeth. Don't you thank Bubba's kind of cute? Somebody told me he's got a real nice trailer." "Oh, I don't know, Lerlene. I guess he's kind of cute, but I had a friend in Dyersburg who went out with him one time, and she said he was kind of stuck up 'cause his daddy got so rich off the bait shop. Say, did you read in the paper the other day about that woman who crawled inside the dishwasher and turned it on and killed herself? I just can't imagine anybody doin' somethin' like that. I had a cousin that used to wash her turnip greens in the dishwasher, but I ain't never heard of nobody crawlin' in one to kill themself. I worry about this neighbor of mine, 'cause she's real depressed all the time 'cause her husband ran off with some dancer from the Whirlaway Club out on the lake. But she couldn't get in no dishwsher to kill herself. Ever since that old two-timer left her, all she's done is eat, eat, eat. She eats all the time. Reba at the beauty shop told me she eats a pound of bacon ever mornin' and then goes down to the coffee shop and gets half-a-dozen glazed donuts and says that she's takin' 'em to her momma, but I know she's not 'cause I have a friend who works with her momma at the factory and she says she ain't never seen her bring any donuts down there to her. Say, speakin' of eatin', I'm gettin' kind of hungry myself. How much longer do we have to sit in here?" "I don't know, Betty Lou, I guess till we figure out whether or not this senator stole that money from that butcher. Why don't you go over and wake Bubba up and ask him how he wants us to vote? I just want to hurry up and get out of here so we can go down to that Peabody hotel and see them little ducks that come down off the elevator and walk down that red carpet to the fountain." "Ducks ridin' an elevator in a hotel and walkin' down a red carpet? Now, what bridge salesman told you about that? I swear, Lerlene, you'd believe anything. Now, get over there and wake up Bubba so we can get out of here."... And so it goes. It's a good thing they decided that people from Shelby County weren't capable of giving Ford a fair trial, or else there's no telling what would have happened...

March 10–16, 1994

One Shining Moment

Life can be so unfair. State Senator John Ford being persecuted by those nasty old state troopers. That insufferable Nancy Kerrigan becoming a multimillionaire just because she got beat up and then went on to come in second place in her Olympic category. Cher putting on all that weight despite the fact that she chooses Equal. Laws that actually allow Dan Quayle to run for president in 1996. It all just becomes too horrible to bear. But then, one day, something happens that makes you believe that, yes, there is justice in the world. Several times in this space I've mentioned a letter I received some time ago, which stated, very simply, "Dear Tim, Go F–k Yourself. Love, A Republican." Well, now the anonymous Republican letter-writer has been outed. And is this ever a great catfight. It seems that said writer was a high-school student at Immaculate Conception at the time, and an I.C. Deep Throat decided to let me know just who I was dealing with. Here are just a few of the comments Deep Throat had to make about writer number one: "She invited Rush Limbaugh to the prom. She worked for over a year at the Raleigh Springs Mall. She is a Civil War re-enactor. She has, on more than one occasion, called my neighborhood [Central Gardens] 'the ghetto.' Like she can talk. She lives behind Piggly Wiggly and a bowling alley in East Memphis. Her family has a fondness for Disney World." Meeeeowwwww! Tonya Harding and Nancy, step aside. And it gets even better. The letter goes on to say, "She was on the Rush radio show and made a fool of herself. She invited Rush, his call screener, and his broadcast engineer to graduation. She sends money to Bob Dole. She screams 'State of the Damned!' when going into Arkansas [the one good thing about her so far]. She made a really tacky 'Rush Is Right' shirt using cheap iron-on letters. She does not read the *Flyer* because it is a 'liberal publication.' She has been known to spend weeks composing letters to cancel her subscriptions to teen magazines listing everything she finds offensive about them. She is not polite, and can't spell well (well, I can't either, but that's not the issue)." Nonsense, honey. There's not one misspelled word or any grammatical errors in your letter at all. And even if there were, I'd still hire you tomorrow. Finished? Hardly. "She likes to do Ross Perot imitations when ordering at drive-in windows. She has no fashion sense. She picked up her date for the Harvest Dance at the Mid-South Fair. Her grandparents sold their tractor to buy her a car, which she totaled a week later leaving a Republican rally. I don't know about now, but as of August she was driving around with tags that had expired in March. She once ran around the airport in sock feet. She has a wall of stuffed animals in her room. Every time she goes over a state border she picks up her feet. She was one of those people who walks around the Memphis in May Barbecue Festival putting stickers on people. I hate that. She has split ends. She looks like Kermit the Frog in pictures. She wrote such sayings as 'It's a conservative throw-down!' and 'I think I'll give up paying taxes for Lent' all over my 1993 calendar. I've run out of things to say about her, but if I think of any more I'll write again. Love, a Democrat." And there you have it. For one brief moment my faith in humanity has been restored. There is poetry in life. There is justice. And there is someone whom I can depend on to take over writing this column when I finally leave this place and move to a civilized country...

May 12–18, 1994

No Dumping

Okay. I'm home from Los Angeles for one day. The city everyone loves to hate. "Oh, it's so gross out there and so nasty and everybody's so rude and shallow," nearly everyone likes to whine. So I go out there, have a nice time, everyone is friendly, and all in all it is a very enjoyable trip (except for being accidently shoved into someone in a crowded club only to learn, as I turned around to say excuse me, that it was Geraldo Rivera —- gag). And the first morning that I'm home, I make my usual daily stop to buy cigarettes and gas, and at the gas station/convenience store/car wash there is a big argument going on in the parking lot between the store manager and who I assume is an agitated patron. The store manager is reading this man the riot act, and the man is yelling back, "If you don't like it, just clean it up yourself." Clean it up yourself? Has the man dropped the gas nozzle and caused a spill? Has he thrown trash out of his car into the parking lot? What is this screaming about? So I go in to get my three packs of generic Basic Best Buy Eagle American Doral Light 100s, and the arguing men carry the fight inside. As it turns out, the "patron" had requested the rest-room key, but the rest room was out of order. So he took it upon himself to simply wander into the drive-through car wash, squat down, and take a dump! Right there with those big scary roller things just flapping away, giving a whole new meaning to the idea of using a bidet. Somehow, the manager, er, caught wind of what was going on, and ran outside to stop the man. Stop the man? I'm thinking to myself, how exactly does one go about this? Someone is in the process of defecating in a drive-through car wash, and you run out and...well, it's still beyond my grasp. Thank God. So anyway, the man then demands to buy gas (no pun intended), and the manager is pretty hot under the collar, and he's telling the man he won't sell it to him. And the man is yelling, "I'm a customer! I'm a customer! It was a 'mergency! It was a 'mergency!" And

I'm thinking, right, Los Angeles is such a pit. I'm so glad to be back in the civilized world. Fortunately, while in line listening to this war that's being waged, I spot the newest issue of the *Weekly World News*, whose front-page headline reads, "BIBLE PRAYERS TO FLUSH OUT BODY FAT: Holy Scriptures show you how to lose weight fast!" Naturally, I am elated and I buy the periodical, wondering, of course, if the man was praying as he was flushing out his body in the car wash. I guess if anything he was praying that a car wouldn't come through there while he was tending to his 'mergency. Anyway, despite this fabulous scenario that's going on, I start to feel kind of depressed about being back home. You know how it is. You go somewhere fun and exciting, and then you come home and get off that plane and head for the house and you're driving through that melange of billboards advertising all of the nearby topless clubs, and you kind of wonder why the hell you came back. So I'm thumbing though the *WWN*, perusing the fascinating mix of articles — "Juggler Busted for Tossing Midget"; "Cybill Shepherd: I Like Men — but I'd Rather Have a Wife"; "Sicko Blinds 4 People — With an Acid- Squirting Bow Tie!"; "Turnip Juice Cures Baldness (at this point I'm wondering what time Easy Way opens)"; and my personal favorite, "I Climbed a Matterhorn — In High Heels and a Cocktail Dress!," which included this quote from the fashion-conscious climber. "I'm appalled when I see mountain climbers dressed in those horrid parkas and clodhopper boots." Amen, sister — even though the article did state that she suffered frost-bitten toes and dehydration. Anything for fashion, I say. Anyway, not only am I depressed about being home, but I'm feeling even lower because I don't get to work for this paper. So I keep flipping through the pages, and lo and behold if there's not an article in the *WWN* titled "How to Stop Feeling Sorry for Yourself — and Turn Life into a Nonstop Party!" Unfortunately, however, the little self-help guide was somewhat off the mark. For instance, the "top psychiatrist" who offers his advice says that one remedy for self-pity is to "Widen your circle of friends. People who have a bigger social network usually are better at handling life's crises. They also lead more exciting lives, because they have a variety of interesting people to interact with!" Please. Anyone who didn't just fall off a turnip-juice truck knows that "networking" is one of the more unabashedly disgusting things in life, enjoyed only by pathetic types who need constant ego-boosting from other pathetic types who are just as gross in their way. The very thought of networking, in fact, makes me—to borrow a phrase I heard recently—shake like a dog and try to shit a peach pit. I tried to network at a convention recently, because I had to,

and ended up being consoled by a friend at 3 a.m. at a place called
Bubba's Barbecue Box. I say, have two or three very good friends, to
whom you can bitch in all sincerity about being old and fat and broke, and
forget the rest of society's barnacles. The more friends you have, the more
inane sob stories you have to be deluged with on a daily basis, and who
needs that? Especially when you know that their lives couldn't possibly be
as rivetingly miserable as your own. Top Shrink then goes on to advise that
to help you stop feeling sorry for yourself, "Don't dwell on your
shortcomings. Think of your strengths. It will boost your self-esteem and
keep you in a party mood all the time!" Right. This, of course, only applies
to the "self-affirmation" crowd, those people who get up every morning
and chant positive things about themselves in the bathroom mirror, like, "I
am worthy. I am a child of the universe. Just like the trees and the stars, I
have a right to be here." In other words, disparingly naive fools. In my
humble opinion, it is much better to be honest and, if you're forced to
even catch a glimpse of yourself in the bathroom mirror in the morning,
say to yourself, "Oh, God. What the hell has gravity done to me?" And, "No
wonder when I walk into a place and people look at my eyes, they tell me
to put my bags over there in the corner." And, "Why exactly is it that I
appear to be disfigured, when I've never before been the victim of any
sort of illness or accident?" But then, maybe this guy is on to something in
regard to concentrating on one's strengths. I'll at least give it a try. Let's
see. (I'm now in front of the bathroom mirror.) 1) I do, at least, have the
depth to fully appreciate the fact that a woman climbed a steep mountain
in high heels and a cocktail dress; others would merely dismiss this as
sheer whimsy, when I have the intelligence to comprehend that this is
history in the making. 2) I am not an overly jealous person. Yes, when I
saw a clip on *Talk Soup* the other day and saw a woman who had a
collection of potato chips in the shape of celebrities, I admit I felt the
undeniable urge to covet and own them, but I didn't become bitter about
it. Even when she pulled out the chip that was a spitting image of Pia
Zadora. That kind of emotional control, I wager to guess, is not something
about which just anyone can openly and honestly boast. And...well, I guess
that's it. I can't think of anything else at the moment, but I'm sure some
little overlooked quality will come to me any minute...

September 22–28, 1994

A Reason to Get out of Bed

 It went something like this: "You $@&-ing bitch! You four-eyed, bug-eyed, wall-eyed stupid crazy bitch!! I'll kick your nappy old fat ass up and down this street, you #$%#-ing crazy stupid fat-ass stinkin' bitch!!" I hate to speak in such vulgar tones, but I'm only relaying the very first thing I heard this morning. In fact, it was so loud it awakened me from a dead sleep. It was one of my lovely neighbors, screaming at top volume. Naturally, I rushed to the door to see what was the matter, expecting to see him pulverizing his wife, but instead, he was in his front yard yelling at a tree. Staring directly at it, his face maybe six inches from it. A tree. This went on most of the morning: coming back and letting the tree have it again. This was all taking place in the Cooper-Young neighborhood where I live, and just happened to be on the day of the Cooper-Young Festival. You have no idea how tempted I was to sneak down and put a big sign in his yard that read "Tour Home — Free Admission." And all of this was just on the heels of yesterday, when, once again, as I attempted to walk out and get in my car, there was a man a few doors down urinating on the sidewalk. I swear I'm not making this up. Just after lamenting in last week's column about how people constantly feel compelled to urinate or defecate in public when I'm around, I see a guy peeing on the sidewalk close enough to my house to hit it if he'd had a mind to, and just weeks after another neighbor pulled up and let two live goats out of the trunk of his car. Ah, the joys of living in Midtown. Wouldn't trade it for any other place in Memphis. And believe me, it could be a lot worse. What if I lived near that bridge over the Wolf River, where a man the other day had to be talked out of jumping from it, shortly after he had left his house where, according to relatives, he'd been breaking

bottles with his head. Luckily, he gave himself up, once his girlfriend got there and offered him some lasagna — and a peach. And this was just one day after a man in the DeSoto County Jail tried to hang himself with a noose made out of torn-up sheets. *The Commercial Appeal*'s headline read, "Man tied to Owens tried to kill self, jailers say." Well, I guess that if I was tied up to Danny Owens I'd be thinking about buying the farm myself. He ought to be glad he wasn't in a Hungarian prison, where he could be locked up with a cellmate who might be a booty-pest. (And you thought I'd sunk as far as I could go.) I know, I know. Suicide and mental illness are not things to make fun of, but...oh, to hell with it. A man breaking bottles over his head and then being talked out of jumping from a bridge by being offered a peach? I'm sorry, but the only thing I can think of is, what a fruit. A man shouting "You crazy fat-ass bitch" at a tree at 7:00 in the morning? Finally, a reason to get out of bed. This is almost as good as what a friend of mine saw at the McDonald's on Union the same day: a woman involved in a heated argument with a cardboard Ronald McDonald cut-out. And what about the entire state of Virginia, where voters have to choose between either Oliver North or Charles Robb, Linda Bird Johnson's husband, in an upcoming Senate race? Linda Bird, who, I might add, has been walking around wearing a flashing red button that she says stands for "My Heart Throbs for Robb." I bet it wasn't throbbing too much for old Chuck when he was caught in that New York hotel room with a naked Miss Virginia. And I say, what's so wrong with that? If Marion Barry can be captured on film smoking crack with a prostitute and then two years later be re-elected as mayor of the nation's capital, then one little tryst with a naked beauty pageant contestant shouldn't be such a big deal. But you know how Puritan some people can be. They just don't know how to have fun...

August 4–10, 1994

Toothless Wonders

Stop the presses. I take back every bad thing I've ever said about Memphis. Well, almost everything; that stunt those political candidates pulled the other day when they flew planes with campaign banners around the Mud Island Amphitheatre, thereby drowning out the concert that was going on, was just about the most stupid thing I've ever heard of. Nevertheless, I have a whole new appreciation for Memphis, now that I've visited a place that makes Frayser seem like the lower East Village. Recently, I had the opportunity to visit the metropolis of Shreveport, Louisiana (if you're from Shreveport and damn proud of it, you may want to stop reading now). Shreveport, I thought, without really thinking, is in Louisiana, like New Orleans, so how bad can it be? Yes, it's smaller and it's up in the northwest corner of the state near — gag— Texas, but it's bound to have some of that funky Cajun charm. Funk? Yes. Charm? Does the name Millington ring a bell? We were greeted in Shreveport by a stop at a convenience store just around the corner from the new apartment of the friend I went to visit, where there was a big freezer where one could, if one had the inclination to do so, purchase "hog maws, pig ears, and chicken necks." Not exactly fresh crawfish and oyster po-boys, but we forged on in search of civilization nonetheless, all the time wondering, naturally, exactly what a "hog maw" was. The mother of a hog? Who knows? Anyway, the search then carried us into downtown Shreveport, whose skyline resembles that of Methodist Hospital Central in Memphis, and which, upon close inspection, looks not altogether unlike our own beautiful Main Street Mall, only about 100 times worse, if you can fathom that. There might be even more wig shops and cheap clothing stores than we have. And no place to stop in for a quick game of pool or cheeseburger or anything like that. So we then decided that, for entertainment, we'd better go ahead and take advantage of the fact that Shreveport has two new casinos right in town. Well, you can imagine the brain trust operating in there. All I can think of to say about that is, Whew! The air of desperation was overwhelming; the atmosphere, something Fellini couldn't have comprehended. After that enriching experience, we then set out again, this time determined that we were going to find a fun little place with pizza, a pool table, and a jukebox — and, hopefully, a few entities that could be loosely described as human beings. I guess we were being overly optimistic. After going from one corner of town to the other, we finally came upon a place that at least looked like it might have some character. There was, after all, a groovy early-1960s convertible T-bird parked at the front door, and the neon sign looked like something from Route 66. Why it didn't hit us, however, that a place called "The Rebel Inn" was going to be somewhat lacking in a progressive clientele, I'm not quite sure. I, for one, was still dizzy from the noise level and the flashing lights of the casino, I guess, and starvation was beginning to take its toll. Upon entering, the three of us were greeted with hooting and screams of laughter from the eight or so people in the place. Did we have boogers hanging out of our noses? No. When we offered a puzzled look, someone shouted, "God dang! We ain't seen nobody in here under 40 in years! Have y'all got all yur teeth, too?!!" Another round of screaming laughter from the tiny crowd, at which time we figured we'd better join in, lest the hoods and sheets come out. So we cracked up along with them, and sat down in a booth, above which there was a tiny mural of a Union soldier saying, "Ah, let's just forget it," and a Confederate soldier replying, "Forget, hell!" This was between two windows draped with Confederate flag curtains. Nice touch. Once our eyes adjusted to the light, we were able to get a better look at the crowd. I cannot find words in the English language to describe the hairstyles being sported by the women. The collective height and volume far exceeded that of Shreveport's tallest building and the colors were ones certainly not found anywhere in nature. Then, whether or not one had all of one's teeth continued to be the running theme of the evening, as none of the other patrons actually had all of theirs, which explains why we were indeed such a novelty. One man, who of course latched onto us immediately — coming over to tell us jokes that all began with the phrase, "Didya hear the one about the nigra feller?" and referring to the casino we'd just come from as, "Oh, the black boat" — did have all of his bottom

45

teeth, and proceeded to show us precisely how fast he could take them in and out, using his tongue to move them about and create a fast clicking sound, similar to someone playing spoons. I feel certain this is something he had practiced until he got it down to an art, and used it regularly as a pick-up device — and it probably works. I kept waiting for him to say to one of us, "You shore gotta purty mouth," but he was so taken with his own teeth-removal tricks and his "nigra feller" jokes that I guess it never occurred to him. Finally, we left The Rebel Inn and the little "clan" of toothless locals, and then we soon left Shreveport. At approximately 100 miles per hour. And I can honestly say that I've never been so glad to see the Memphis skyline in my life...

August 25–31, 1994

Mudbug Madness

Some people just have no sense of humor. Not to mention anything better to do than sit around fretting about what they read in this thing every week. All in one fell swoop, I suddenly have the mayor of Shreveport, Louisiana, writing me letters in response to some things I wrote a few weeks ago about her city, and inviting me to come back for another visit; and members of Bellevue Baptist Church writing to tell me that they are praying for me and inviting me to come to their church and see what it's really all about. Shreveport and Bellevue Baptist. Do I really deserve such good fortune? All I said about Shreveport was that I'd been there, it was kind of yucky, there wasn't an awful lot to do, and that I wound up in a place where the people got a kick out of our teeth and where one man in particular took a liking to us and let us in on his litany of "nigra feller" jokes — which, I might add, was all true. So Mayor Hazel Beard, after somehow obtaining a copy of that week's *Flyer*, sent me a nice letter diplomatically retaliating against my comments, informing me that yes, there were myriad things to do in Shreveport, and that I should come back and have a native of the city take me around to some of the more exciting events, like the annual "Mudbug Madness Festival" and the "Great Louisiana Hayride." Well, Hazel, I suppose I spoke too soon, didn't I? I'll just cancel that trip I was planning to the south of France and head straight down and help the fine folks of your fine city celebrate the "Mudbug." Hazel did make the astute observation that if I were to take a good look around Memphis, I would likely find plenty of places just like the one in Shreveport where whether or not one had all of one's teeth was the ongoing theme of the conversation. And I guess she's got me there. And I guess if one is from Memphis, one has no valid reason for throwing stones at other cities. After all, on my own street, some neighbors pulled up the other day and let two goats out of the trunk of their car. It seems they had something to do with a wedding ceremony. As for Bellevue, I don't even remember what I said — something about brainwashing and the architectural style of their facility — but I'm sure it wasn't enough to get them all riled up and into a praying fit. But I guess it doesn't take much. Still, I say, if y'all want to pray, pray for those who really need it. Pray for people who wear "I'm with stupid" T-shirts. Or pray for people who talk on cellular phones while eating out in restaurants. Or pray for Valerie Bertinelli to retire from show business. Or pray that there are no more tornados or divorces in Frayser, so that no one else has to go through the trauma of losing a trailer home. Or pray for the toothless people in Shreveport; maybe they'll suddenly wake up with a full set of choppers, or at least an image of the Virgin Mary — or Elvis — on the palms of their hands. Or pray for the nursing-home residents who, according to a newspaper article I read the other day, are finding themselves not so ready to meet their maker because they're so enthralled by the O.J. Simpson case. I speak the truth. It seems that in nursing homes around the country, residents who really had no motivation to keep on living are now bouncing back and defying ill health and death so they can be around to see the outcome of O.J.'s trial. Only in America. And do they ever have something to look forward to. That same newspaper reported that O.J. has a new alibi he's about to come out with when he finally goes to trial: that he was at Denny's that night and had to wait there for six hours until someone finally served him! (I guess now I'll get a letter from Denny's inviting me to come disguised as a black person and find that they indeed do not discriminate.) Shreveport, Bellevue Baptist, and Denny's. What more could I ask for? Somehow, the word lobotomy comes immediately to mind. But I guess I'll never be that lucky...

December 23–30, 1995

Ducks on Speed

My life is *so* exciting. At the moment, I am staring at the television guide trying to decide whether to watch *The Bad News Bears Go to Japan* or *Emmet Otter's Jug Band Christmas Show*. This is, of course, after watching several hours of cooking shows, playing "dry the cat's head" with a beach towel and my cat, trying not to vomit after accidentally watching 30 seconds of a Peter, Paul, & Mary holiday concert, and then roasting a chicken. All of which was a desperate attempt to not go Christmas shopping. But, in the end, I had to buckle down and go. And was it ever fun. First stop: Target. Where else? At Target, I wander aimlessly around for at least an hour, without a clue as to exactly what I am doing there. Finally, to keep from looking too suspect, not to mention insane, I put a coffee-bean grinder in the basket. Then I call my mother from the Target Guest Service desk, at which time I am informed that she already purchased a coffee-bean grinder for my brother. So I have to put it back. And wander around for another hour. Then I have a very stimulating conversation with a salesperson about a battery-operated talking parrot. She acts as if this is an automobile I am about to buy, explaining in detail the many things this parrot is capable of. I feel so guilty about taking up her time that I actually put the parrot into the basket and walk around for a while longer, then, when I'm sure she's not looking, I sneak around and put it back on the shelf. I am sincerely afraid that she might start crying if she sees that I'm not going to buy the parrot. So. I'm at Target, I've been at Target for at least two hours, and I am still pushing around an empty basket. I am about to start crying myself. Christmas carols are blaring, the store is so crowded that I can barely maneuver, and I completely understand why certain people commit mass murders in these kinds of situations. So I think to myself, I'll at least put a carton of cigarettes into the basket. I know I'm going to buy them before I leave, and that will be *something* in the basket so that I don't continue wandering around with an empty one. At this point I am very paranoid. Well, guess what: They don't sell cigarettes any more, I am informed by yet another enthusiastic salesperson. I think she tells me they've stopped selling cigarettes because they have had so many "cigarette deaths," which I think is not only an odd comment, but an odd reason to stop selling them. But she repeats her statement, and as it turns out, it is because they've had so many "thefts." Much more reasonable. But I still have an empty basket. I suddenly have a revelation: One of my brothers and his wife have recently set up a very elaborate aquarium. I will buy them fish things. I go to the Guest Services center and call my mother. She tells me not to buy fish things, because the aquarium is done in certain colors, and whatever I buy will probably not match. I want to kill myself. I didn't even know that aquariums were decorated with color schemes. I just thought they had little fish castles and rocks and fake plants. But no. My mother had mentioned "mauve" in the conversation, and I am now having a complete breakdown. Several hours later, I finally leave Target. I have purchased a Crayola Crayon school bus, some sort of Mickey Mouse pillow, and a wooden spoon. The cashier has placed these items in commemorative *It's a Wonderful Life* paper bags, though I don't realize this until I'm getting into the car in the parking lot and it is too late to slug her in the head with the Crayola Crayon bus. As I finally crank the car and prepare to leave, I reach into my pocket for a cigarette, and, naturally, I am out. It is not yet noon, and already I am trying to think of ways to make my death look accidental so the insurance company will pay off and I won't leave my family stuck with a lot of debt. As I pull the car out of the parking spot to leave, I hear a sort of thud on the back of the car. I get out and realize that in the mad dash to get the hell out of this place, I have left the Crayola Crayon bus on top of the car and it is now lying in the parking lot — in several pieces. I blame this all on my brothers for having children. Are they out going through this kind of torture to buy gifts for my cat? No. They are probably at home, resting and having a nice time. I finally make it to a convenience store to buy cigarettes, and I contemplate finishing my Christmas shopping here. There is a nice selection of hats, one of which is emblazoned with the phrase "Go Hogs!" There is also a case of extremely attractive watches. One of them appears to be a mood watch with a picture of a unicorn on it. I begin to convulse. I suddenly — and vividly —

recall being at some sort of craft store a few days earlier, where I saw a pen-and-pencil desk set, the base of which was, in fact, a piece of heavily varnished wood on which was decoupaged a photo-illustration of Naomi and Wynonna Judd. I begin to wonder if there is a God. Weeks ago, I was walking along the moonlit canals of Amsterdam and watching as wild geese flew overhead and landed gracefully in a river in Hyde Park in London. And now I am reliving looking at Naomi and Wynonna Judd decoupaged onto a piece of wood, not to mention browsing through unicorn-decorated watches and hats that say "Go Hogs!" And I haven't had a cigarette in several hours, as I've been at Target talking to a quite chipper young woman about a battery-operated talking parrot. I try to think of positive things, like, at least I don't live in West Memphis, and I'm not wearing adult diapers, yet. But it does no good. As if to add insult to injury, I catch myself humming a Christmas carol. I don't even know what it is, but I suspect it's one of the two or three thousand I've heard at Target earlier. I slap myself and feel better. I check the two radio stations my AM car radio can pick up, and finally hear a Barry White song. I have hope. Until, that is, I make the mistake of popping into the flea market. The first sight I am confronted with here is that of a huge display of those hand-painted wooden ducks, with their wings whirling like mad in circles in the wind. There appear to be hundreds of these ducks. They look like they are under the influence of amphetamines. And they are scaring me. I recoil in horror and walk in the other direction. I desperately want a Pronto Pup, but I remember that I've recently become a vegetarian in a futile attempt to lose weight. I continue to consider getting the Pronto Pup, knowing that I'll probably throw up anyway after I eat it. But I resist. I walk past a booth in which a woman is sitting and painting on old pieces of wood. She is actually painting the words "Gone Fishin" in a very rustic style of lettering on these pieces of wood. This makes me again think of the Naomi and Wynonna Judd desk set, and again I begin to shake. I wonder about the possible benefits of creative visualization, but I can't make myself believe in it. And besides, every time I close my eyes I see the unicorn mood watch. I consider running as fast as I can to my car, but somehow gather the wherewithal to stay and continue shopping. I walk past several booths which offer a variety of hand-made wood products, such as heart-shaped plant stands and Taters N' Stuff storage bins. I consider purchasing the plant stand, but I collect myself and realize that I cannot support this movement and maintain a clear conscience. I stop and think, "When did I ever have a clear conscience?" But I still pass on the country-kitchen plant stand. In the next area, a man is selling big jars of sorghum and metal buckets filled with dried flower arrangements. I stare in disbelief and walk on. I briefly consider converting to the Jehovah's Witness religion, but that would mean joining an organization and socializing, and I simply don't do either. Besides, who wants to have a Jehovah's Witness already in the house? I try to cheer myself up by thinking of the time I walked into a small grocery store/bait shop in Mississippi one late night around Christmastime, and was greeted by an elderly woman behind the counter, who was wearing a Santa Claus hat and picking hairs from her nose with a pair of tweezers. I am momentarily entertained, but at that precise moment someone grazes my ankle with a baby stroller. Finally, and empty-handed, I leave the premises of the beautiful Mid-South Fairgrounds. I get home and check the mail. First, there's a $156 utility bill. I live in a four-room house. Then there is a barrage of Christmas cards. One is from a friend in New York, who informs me in the card that he has just moved into a building which has a doorman. I am very happy for him. There is another, which is printed on recycled paper. I think of the Judd desk set, and wonder why people even bother. Finally, there is one from a very dear friend. On the front of the card there's a picture of a very sheepish-looking reindeer passing gas, with the letters "pfffft" coming out of its little reindeer behind. On the inside is the holiday greeting, "Do you hear what I hear?" I feel much better…

September 24–30, 1992

Sperm in Space

What a week. They're playing with sperm in space, Ross Perot's intolerable mug is back in the picture, they finally crowned a Miss America who didn't use the answer "world peace" to the big final question, and Phyllis Schlafly's son burst forth from the closet and admitted to being a homosexual. Maybe now that heinous old bag will keep her trap shut. Not that anyone with an I.Q. higher than that of a lima bean ever paid any attention to her. My week, as if anyone cares, has been rather event-filled itself. Let's see. It all started when I had to attend a 7:30 a.m. breakfast attended mostly by important businesspersons, philanthropists, and other types who somehow have the enthusiasm to look forward to the opportunities presented by each new day. Of course, as soon as I walked in, someone had the discreet tact to point out that there was a flea crawling around on my forehead. Little did I know that, even worse, I had washed a red sheet — for the first time — that I've had on my bed for what seems like months (probably because it has) and, never one to become bogged down with tiresome details like sorting, threw it in the washer with everything else. To make a long story short, not only was there a flea on my forehead but I was also wearing pink underwear. The breakfast lasted an hour and a half and I was not allowed to smoke. Nice, huh? Too bad I can't do that every morning. Between that and my morning ritual of cleaning up hairballs (the cat's, not mine), perhaps I could finally attain my life's ambition: to retire and live off disability checks merited by a mental condition that renders me totally unable to cope with the simplest aspects of life. But I guess I'll have to wait a few years until incontinence sets in and I'm found rummaging through garbage cans for empty Mrs. Weaver's containers and old copies of the *Weekly World News*. "A few" being the key phrase in that sentence. I did, however, get to speak in a very scary, harsh manner to a couple of kids this week, which kind of made up for the rest of the excruciating chain of events, which, by the way, included getting a very urgent-sounding message from someone at the Butterball Turkey National Hotline. With Thanksgiving not too, too far away, I'll be sure to find that number and list it here just in case any of you have a turkey emergency and need to speak with one of their counselors. ("Now, try to calm down. What exactly are you feeling about this turkey trauma? Put down that baster and get in touch with your emotions. Go ahead, don't be afraid to cry. Are you having problems stuffing the turkey, or are you really just transferring your anger and stuffing your true feelings? Is it rubbing the salt into the bird's cavity that makes you frightened?") Then, I got a piece of mail soliciting my membership in a club that publishes a magazine designed to answer all sorts of difficult questions, including: A) What should you do if you're locked out of a room in an expensive European hotel room — naked?; B) Why do dogs bark?; C) Why did the U.S. Supreme Court decide that the tomato is a vegetable, not a fruit? (one can only assume that they couldn't think of anything better to worry about that day); and D) Why was a museum in Denmark built entirely with Lego bricks? At that point, things were beginning to look up. But then I received an invitation to a "media workout" at a local spa, to which it was requested that I wear Spandex. If that wasn't an encouraging portent that the end of the world has got to be right around the corner, I don't know what is. But who knows when that will finally be...

September 9–16, 1993

Thanks for Nothing

Last night I saw a woman violently bludgeoned to death, was almost bitten by a pair of big green dogs who had the heads of whales, and found myself hanging from the top of a 40-story building, trying to lasso a giant glass of Windex on the sidewalk below. Then I finally woke up. Exhausted, of course. Actually, this is nothing unusual. I'm one of those people who dreams vivid, technicolor, hallucinatory dreams nearly every night. I have to wake up to rest. Sometimes I wake up talking, and sometimes laughing. Whatever the case, I'm usually in a state of sheer panic. I sleepwalk, and get up and get dressed for work from time to time before realizing that it's only 3 a.m. I even cooked a pot of rice in my sleep one night — and it didn't stick. I'd be a shrink's dream, but I don't see one. Not anymore. I stopped seeing them years ago after deciding that watching reruns of *Phyllis* was much more therapeutic. As are snapping beans, bonding with the cat, and any number of other things that you can do in the privacy of your own home at no cost and without any grief. Which, believe me, you get plenty of at the doc's. For one thing, you can't smoke in most psychiatrists' offices anymore. Isn't that brilliant? They want you to drop a hundred bucks an hour to relive every horror you've ever been through, get rebirthed, get hypnotized, talk about how you secretly hate your family, cry, scream, and talk to empty chairs, but you can't light up a cigarette? Very therapeutic. It would be easier to just go ahead and have the hole drilled in your head and forget everything. And what is all this jazz about "getting in touch with your feelings"? That's all you ever hear out of psychiatrists these days. To which I reply, I feel like crap! And you're charging me a hundred bucks an hour and not letting me smoke to sit here and tell me I need to try to feel more of this? Pardon my stupidity, but I thought I was here to make this go away. Thanks. Thanks for nothing. And even worse than the psychiatrists are the "therapists," you know, the ones who took the correspondence course in self-help language. The last time I saw one of them, his incredibly valuable advice was to have me go home and write down "five positive things about myself" and bring them to the next session. Which, of course, I had to postpone for several months while trying to finish the list. If he had tried to make me say them in the mirror every morning, I would have pulled a loaded weapon on him. And then there are those who think every problem is an extension of something that happened to you as a small child. They want you to think back as far as you possibly can, so you can figure out what's wrong with you now. Right. I really don't think being thousands of dollars in debt, having a hideous job, being stressed out 24 hours a day, being in a rotten marriage, and having to avoid the IRS at all times is any direct result of something Mr. Music might have said on *Romper Room*. And then there are the label doctors. The ones with cute little names for every imaginable diagnosis. You're worried about someone you care about because he or she is being held hostage in a foreign country and tortured with burning cigarettes or by being forced to watch interviews with Richard Simmons? Nonsense. You're not a caring person. You're just being "co-dependent." Enjoy the physical contact between you and your "significant other?" Nonsense. You're a "sex addict." What ever happened to the good old days when people were loony, psychotic, neurotic, paranoid, schizophrenic, and just plain nuts? No wonder crime is on the rise. If the doctors out there would just tell their patients that they're wacko and that there's no hope of them ever functioning properly in society again, maybe they'd stay home, take their medication, and mind their own business. But nooooooooo, today's mental-health practitioner wants to "heal" everyone. Make them productive. Give them a new sense of self-worth. Wonder how many of these people David Koresh visited until he finally went off the deep end? If only he could have gone on *Oprah* and purged himself in front of the masses. But he didn't and now he's dead and who really cares? Not me. And hopefully not you...

December 17–23, 1992

The Real Shocker

Unless your intellectual aspirations are to be as smart as, say, Bo Derek, then you've probably figured out that this is a special issue of the *Flyer*, marking its 200th week of publication. A bicentennial celebration of sorts. A fond glance back at the last nearly-four years. Notations of things such as the fall of the Berlin Wall, four horrid years of George Bush, wars declared for no sensible reason, pyramids built for less sensible reasons, new mayors, old arguments, and other milestones that have been covered along the way. Well, all this means to me is that I've had to write this column 200 times! That's approximately 40,000 words, 40,000 words which have caused an invisible neon sign to appear across my forehead, beckoning every looney-tune around to call me, write to me, approach me in public, and generally do things that have cost me a sizeable sum of money doled out to a succession of therapists — all to minimal avail. I've had death threats. I was stalked before being stalked was cool. I've had letters saying that finding something to do in this column is like trying to find something to eat in a garbage dumpster. Letters calling me an asshole, a communist, a liar, a hack, a psycho. . . and a few other choice things that I'll refrain from stating here. And all because I've said one or two controversial things. Go figure. And then there are the letters that simply appear out of nowhere, in response to nothing, for no apparent reason. A letter from an 85-year-old, who enclosed a five-page essay — for possible publication — on "society's misunderstanding and persecution of the small penis." And then there were the more recent letters from the man claiming to have murdered someone execution-style for his crimes against humanity. On the same day, I received a letter from a guy who felt compelled to alert me to the fact that he'd been to a local masseur and that "the real shocker came when he felt the masseur's erect penis pressing between his buttocks," and who then went on to tell me how much he enjoyed it (by far my favorite letter so far). And people think this job is glamorous. On the flipside, there have been many very nice letters and calls. One African-American biker in Pennsylvania reads the *Flyer* every week for some reason and occasionally writes to say how much he enjoys this column. A very sweet elderly lady here in Memphis calls every once in a while to tell me she hates George Bush as much as I do. One very nice grocery-store checker tells me her favorite line every week. At one time, there was even a bank teller who'd let me write checks for more money than was in my account if I promised to make a deposit the next day and bring her a copy of the paper early (her I love). And then there are the people who call with events they feel certain should be recommended on this page. A live, big-screen telebroadcast of cataract surgery? I don't think so. A snuff-bottle collectors' conference? Guess I was just too narrow-minded. Spam cook-off? Well, I think that one did find its way in. Must've been a slow week. And speaking of slow weeks, have you any idea of what it's like to recommend 200 weeks' worth of entertainment in a city like Memphis, where the biggest extravaganza of the year is an outdoor hog-cooking contest in 90-degree weather? Let's just say it's a bit like trying to convince the Academy Award judges that Pia Zadora should be taken seriously as a dramatic actress. However, not all has been bad on the entertainment scene for the last 200 weeks. Some congratulations are in order for a few people and organizations who've tried to be creative in bringing us something worthwhile. Michael Powell of Fresh Ideas Productions; the New Daisy Theater; the Memphis Center for Contemporary Art (when it was in business). Preston Johnson's filmfest at Brooks; the Board of the Overton Park Shell; Ambarish Keshani of the Cinema Showcase 8 (formerly the Fare 4); the Vapors Club (where would we be without those Elvis impersonators?); the Apartment Club (where would we be without those female impersonators?); the World Class Jazz series; the National Ornamental Metal Museum; Friends for Life (formerly ATEAC) for the best fund-raisers in town; and Old Zinnie's, just for being there. I'm sure there are more that deserve mention, but I've just about used up all of my available brain cells. What follows was not my idea; some "best of" kind of thing concocted by the staff and chosen by a total stranger. In fact, at this writing, I don't even know what's going to follow. And I don't care. All I know is I've written 200 of these things and this week I'm getting a break. It's about damn time…

on Hate Mail: "I suppose putting up with diatribes from the mayonnaiseon-white-bread nuclear-family set is just part of the price you have to pay when you're a love slave to the bitch goddess known as fame."

on Censorship in Journalism: "People can run around ecstatic about America going to war, eat spicy Cajun barbecued ranch nacho cheese pork rinds like there's no tomorrow, own chihuahuas, belong to all-white country clubs, engage in Civil War-era Cotton Carnival activities, wear clogs, listen to Sandi Patti records, and watch an unlimited number of shows about real-life trailer-park murders, but try to slip a good gerbil joke into print and it's as if you've called the Pope the old fat guy who really runs the Mafia."

on Current Affairs: "What a week. They're playing with sperm in space, Ross Perot's intolerable mug is back in the picture, they finally crowned a Miss America who didn't use the answer 'world peace' to the big final question, and Phyllis Schlafly's son burst forth from the closet and admitted to being a homosexual. Maybe now that heinous old bag will keep her trap shut."

on the Clarence Thomas/Anita Hill Hearings: "Yes, I'm sure Ms. Hill sat up for days reading *The Exorcist* trying to come up with stories . . . to use while perjuring herself on national television. Why, if recalled to the stand, I wouldn't be surprised if she peed on the floor, told the committee that Thomas walked around talking about his mother copulating in hell, swiveled her head around like a Tasmanian devil, made the committee's tables shake around and rise a couple of feet off the floor, and projectile-vomited big blasts of green gook at the committee when re-asked the inane question about why she didn't report this 10 years ago, when it happened."

on Dan Quayle vs. Murphy Brown: "Sure, Quayle publicly blamed the nation's most serious problems on a silly TV show, but it could very well be that he thought he was commenting on a real-life situation . . . Maybe he got the fictionalized TV-sitcom mixed up with the real news and thought that a real-life anchor had chosen to have a baby out of wedlock — say, Connie Chung or even Bryant Gumbel. After all, Bryant does have brown skin and Murphy's last name is Brown."

on Bill Clinton's Appearance on the Arsenio Hall Show: "Anyone who can sit on the same stage with Arsenio Hall without grabbing him by the collar and pounding his face into the wall repeatedly — especially when he starts that obnoxious rolling-his-fist-around-in-the-air motion that looks like some manifestation of untreated Tourette's syndrome — does show a great sense of diplomacy."

on Ross Perot: He's slick, all right. But so is owl feces on a glass doorknob."

on Homosexuals in the Military: "I bet while all the normal guys are out on the battlefield fighting like 'men,' the 'others' will be down in a foxhole, pantomiming Judy Garland's 'The Man Who Got Away' and squealing every time a bullet whizzes past."

on Memphis Race Relations: "The only successfully racially integrated groups in town are the Jehovah's Witnesses and the homeless."

on the Pastie Ordinance: "If indeed 90GGG is the measurement of Lisa Gazombas' breasts, then exactly how much good would it do to put pasties on them? Unless of course, the city council imposes a pastie size ruling. And for a 90GGG, the pastie would have to be something around the size of a satellite dish."

on Local Television: Did anyone see that infamous furniture company's [St. Patrick's Day] commercial with the friendly founder talking about big mcsales on mcsleeper-sofas and mcsectionals? Mcsectionals? One glass of Raid, please."

on TV News: "I got to see one on-the-scene reporter covering a terrible highway accident, about which she commented, 'Police have not been able to identify the body, but they say it's a white male from Mississippi.' Come again? Did they come to that conclusion based on his Budweiser belt buckle?"

on Spring Cleaning: "Normally, I would never participate in anything so civilized or lemming-like, but I got this new piece of furniture and had to clean underneath the old one when making the switch. And underneath this old couch I uncovered the following inventory: numerous Styrofoam packing peanuts, subscription forms to several magazines, Christmas ornaments, a fake cardinal with wire feet, a back issue of the *Weekly World News* whose headline read 'Titanic Victims Speak Through A Waterbed,' socks, rubber bands, lots of fast-food wrappers, enough lint to insulate a small housing development, pens, pencils, matches, countless cigarette packs, leaves, party invitations (oops), a couple of bucks in change, a pile of plastic vomit given to me in a pizza box on my 30th birthday, and several chestnuts. Chestnuts? Who knows."

on Central Hardware's Mr. Tinker Show: "I wonder if they'll have a demonstration booth where someone is sitting with a martini calling a repairman, like any self-respecting person would do?

on Mondays: "Naturally, the only thing Memphis offers on Monday night in the way of entertainment is Championship Wrestling at the Fairgrounds, where you could, if you so choose, go and watch a bunch of barbarians acting out scenes from the Neanderthal age. I refer, of course, to the audience."

on Christmas: "I was going to tell you about the dream I had last night, in which I had several Christmas carolers, mostly children, lined up against a concrete wall at sunrise, blindfolded, with cigarettes quivering in their mouths. But as soon as I did, somebody would come along and actually mow a group of them down and it would just look too suspicious."

on New Year's Eve: "Ah, my favorite night to sit around watching videos and thinking how crummy life is."

on New Year's Resolutions for 1992: "I resolve to buy only the buy-one-get-one free cigarette deals so I can smoke twice as much. I resolve to call an abrupt halt to my rigorous exercise program; all that time I spend lifting coffee cups and walking from my door to my car could be spent on much less narcissistic things. I'm going to stop being such a nice guy; it's time to call a booger a booger and someone has to do it and it may as well be me."

April 27—May 3, 1995

Gone Fishing

I've done it again. Every so often, for some reason, I find myself out in the middle of the countryside. Bonding with the earth. Becoming one with nature. Breathing fresh air. It always makes me a nervous wreck. This time, I was on a fishing trip (yeah, yeah, yeah, a fishing trip; is it that hard to believe?) in a very picturesque setting, off in the mountains on a beautiful river, with the intention of catching trout. Well. The first thing that happens is that the fishing guide starts our tour by telling us all of the ways the boat can turn over in the water. "But don't worry if it does," he continues, "because there's no way you can swim to the bank. The water is too cold and hypothermia will set in immediately." So much for relaxing in the sunshine and enjoying the scenery. I'm on my way to an untimely death. In the middle of nowhere. So we set out, and thankfully it doesn't seem as if the boat is going to sink. We begin to fish. A friend who's with me catches one. Then he catches another. Then the guide catches one. Then the friend catches another. Fishing tales are exchanged. Phrases like "loosen the drag" and "yank the rod with your wrist" are being tossed about. I, of course, am concentrating on the bait we are using: little round orange balls all connected together in one long strand. I'm still not sure if the fishing guide knew what I was talking about when I proclaimed that they looked just like pop beads, that venerable costume-jewelry invention from decades past. Suffice it to say that from the look on his face, I shouldn't have made that particular connection. But I continue putting worms and the pop beads and weights and things on the line and the hook. The friend catches another. The guide catches another. I suddenly feel a big bite. I yank the rod with my wrist. I loosen the drag. It feels like a really big fish. Probably because I have hooked a really big log, which causes my line to break and rips all of the line that is left out of the reel. This is within, oh, 10 minutes of setting out. So the fishing guide gives me another rod. I continue to fish. The fishing guide then begins to tell stories about all the times snakes have fallen out of trees and into the boat. Great. I'm risking drowning, freezing to death, and getting bitten by snakes, and I have caught not one fish. I look around the boat, desperately wishing that it housed a television. I may be in the middle of the beautiful wilderness, but I still would like to watch *I Love Lucy*. Instead, I find myself constantly watching for snakes. I am wearing a pair of black suede shoes from Payless Shoe Source and a borrowed black turtleneck that is too big, and on me looks like more of a cowl neck. Though there is no mirror, I am convinced that I look like Maude. I find comfort only in the fact that I am out on a river where no one can see me. I keep thinking of the movie *Man's Favorite Sport*, in which Rock Hudson has to enter a fishing tournament and pretends he knows what he's doing. He ended up catching fish; what the hell is wrong with me? Can the fish see me in this turtleneck and are they down there laughing? Finally, it happens. I feel a bite. I yank the rod with my wrist. I loosen the drag. I begin to reel it in. It feels like a big one. My rod is bending. The fish is fighting. The line is stretching. I'm reeling with a vengeance. The boat is rocking. The fishing guide is ready with the net. I get the beast near the edge of the boat and pull hard to get him all the way out of the water. It is a trout that is perhaps six inches long. And it is looking right at me. It looks to me like it's in shock. Like it was minding its own business down there in the water, playing with all of the other baby trout, when all of a sudden some wretched human decided it was time to stick a big sharp hook through its mouth. It is writhing around on the end of the line, and I swear it is staring at me and pleading for its life. I feel as if tears are about to well up in my eyes, and ask the fishing guide to quickly get the fish back into the river and let it go. "Yeah," the fishing guide says. "We'd better give him a few more years to grow up." I am humiliated. This happens several times, and I can tell I am going to have nightmares from now on every time I drive past a Captain D's. We finally break for lunch, and I go into a store where a man with bulged-out eyes commences to give me an oral dissertation on the history of grits. "Back to the river!" I demand, and we fish the rest of the day. I come home with a sunburn, a guilt complex, and clothes that smell like Power Bait. I am glad to be home, though I did have a great time, and for one day got to act positively butch. Well, except for the comment about pop beads, I guess...

Oct. 28–Nov. 3, 1993

Queen for a Day

Just when you thought you'd heard everything to make you want to leave America and go live in the middle of the Middle East's hottest desert for the rest of your natural life, along comes this: Iowa City educator Marian Coleman and her Equity-Affirmative Action Advisory Committee sending a note to parents trying to dictate what school kids should and shouldn't dress up as on Halloween. Like I said, you thought you'd heard everything. This is the kind of thing that not only causes permanent psychological problems, but as far as I can tell it's a violation of civil rights. Not that I like Halloween or kids or dressing up in costumes, because I really don't. I am loath even to remotely acknowledge a holiday, much less celebrate one. But hey, I'm a live-and-let-live kind of guy and if people want to take this day as an opportunity to look even more foolish than they already do, it's their business. But not according to Ms. Coleman, who — in an attempt to spare the feelings of racial, ethnic, and other types of groups — is trying to prohibit the little rug rats from dressing as the following: Gypsies, American Indians, old men and women, "differently abled persons" (somebody ought to slap her merely for using that term), slaves, devils, Africans, East Indians, hobos, and princesses. Princesses? Here's a bulletin for you, Marian: You're an idiot. Who the hell is going to be offended by seeing a little girl dressed up like a princess? The Royal Family? I can see parents not wanting their little boys to dress up as queens, but 10 percent of them are going to eventually, so what's the big deal? And what would Halloween be without Gypsies? Every kid dresses up like a Gypsy on one Halloween or another. And who cares what the Gypsies think anyway? All they're good for is stealing babies and selling them and robbing J.B. Hunter stores, when they were still around. And as

64

for nationalities, how did she come to the conclusion that this perceived mockery of dressing up would be offensive only to Africans and East Indians? What about other cultures who've been the butt of society's cruel jokes? Like the Swedish. Those poor people have had to live with the legacy of ABBA for the last 20 years. I say, let the East Indians have it and leave the Swedes alone. They've suffered enough. Even more ludicrous than Coleman's "don't" list is her "do" list. These are the costumes she finds acceptable: friendly monsters, animals, carrots, flowers, pencils (pencils? This woman is working with an I.Q of a manhole cover), pumpkins, and people from history or other eras, such as the roaring '20s. Oh, I get it. It's a slap in the face of humanity to dress up like a princess but it's fine to go out done up as a gangster or a gin-guzzling slut from some 1920s clip joint. Or maybe Hitler: He was someone from history. How about J. Edgar Hoover, speaking of little boys dressing up like queens? And what kid worth his sack full of candy wants to parade around all night dressed as a carrot? He or she might as well just wear a huge sign that says, "I am such an insufferable geek that I decided to dress as a vegetable high in minerals and vitamins that help build strong eyesight. Go ahead and kill me now so I won't grow up to be a sickening adult like that crackpot in Iowa." As usual, being the benevolent soul that I am, I have given some deep thought to this matter and have come up with an alternative list of acceptable and unacceptable costumes for the little kiddies, just to make things easier for them. Not acceptable: Republicans, members of any self-help group, people who for reasons best left unknown feel compelled to rollerblade, members of Citizens Against New Taxes, performance artists, mimes, people with vanity plates, and anyone who wears Spandex in public. These costumes are not unacceptable because they might offend someone; it's just that these particular types of people are already a revolting enough sight, and who wants to see more of them? Acceptable: Joan Rivers, characters from any John Waters movie, *Talk Soup*'s Greg Kinnear, Hillary Clinton, Lorena Bobbitt (but take a fake kitchen knife with you), John Bobbitt (just take one of those fake chopped-off, bloody fingers and blow it up), the woman in California who shot someone in a Denny's for complaining about her cigarette smoke, Cindy Crawford, and Shelley Winters. These we'd like to see more of. Maybe I will dress up this Halloween after all. Let's see: What will I need if I decide to be a one-legged, blind, deaf, poor, homeless, crack-addicted, overweight, black Muslim, bald, vegetarian, epileptic lesbian dwarf?

December 3–9, 1992

A Little Yuletide Cheer

It's already started, and if I have to look at one more friggin' elf, candy
cane, or reindeer, I'm gonna puke. One more "jolly holly" anything, one
more whiff of some nasty potpourri, one more glance at some fat old,
child-molesting loser dressed up as Santa Claus, and one more "news
report" about retail sales, and that's going to be it. Of course, all of this
started back in, oh, about, August, but now the worst is here. And it's
virtually impossible, as far as I can tell, to avoid the inevitable holiday
assault. However, having spent years trying to figure out a way around
this, I have been able to gather a few tips for those who regard Christmas
with about as much anticipation as that burning hemorrhoidal itch. 1)
Carry mace. At all times between now and January. It comes in very handy
if a troupe of carolers should fall into your line of vision, or if some
nincompoop comes to your door trying to sell Christmas cards. And it can
be a lifesaver if you get kidnapped and taken to a mall, where one of those
holiday talent shows is featured on the main stage, which without
question will involve a pack of completely rhythmless white kids trying to
tap dance to some horrid holiday medley. 2) Don't answer the phone.
While this is a good rule of thumb to follow throughout the entire year, it
comes in especially handy now, when out-of-towners who you thought
were mercifully out of your hair forever start popping into town, when
people are calling to invite you to Christmas parties, and the worst: when
people are just in a good mood and want to "share" their holiday joy. If
there was such a thing as phone mace, this particular problem wouldn't
be so bad. Of course, you could just leave a message on your machine
saying, "If your call has anything at all to do with yuletide cheer, I hope
your eyes fall out of their sockets in your sleep," but most people would
probably take that as a joke. 3) Charities. There's no reason to get all
mushy about the woes of the world just because it's the holiday season.

Things stink all year long, so why get all unravelled now? If you want to help the world, take your money and spend it at a psychologist's office to lessen the burden you are on society at large. Better yet, just send big bags of money to me in care of this newspaper. 4) Pets. Do not dress them up in cute little outfits. It's a disgusting sight, and think of how humiliated your animal friends will be. If you have to put something around their necks, pearls, I hear, are still in, though the Barbara Bush choker pearls, according to *The Commercial Appeal*, are out. 5) Christmas trees. Forget it. They're fire hazards and they make horrible messes. And don't buy any of that garbage about it being a okay to chop down trees because now they can be recycled. That's just some play concocted by the people who sell them in the parking lots of strip shopping centers. A tree murder is a tree murder. Not that I'm an environmentalist by any stretch of the imagination; but this save-the-planet philosophy that's become so popular does come in handy within this particular context. 6) *Hallmark Hall of Fame* made-for-TV holiday specials. Avoid them as you would a Jesse Helms fan club party. They are depressingly optimistic and have nothing to do with real life. And just how many times can you take watching Michael Learned staring out a window worried about something that's never quite identified? 7) If all else fails, simply become a Jehovah's Witness. They've got the right idea and once you let your conversion be known, no one will want to talk to you anyway for fear that you'll show up on their doorstep at 8 a.m. on a Saturday with an armful of literature you'd like to go over with them for just a few minutes. Works every time. And there you have the basics. There's no guarantee that these helpful hints will work like magic, but it's a start. If anything else comes to mind during the next few weeks, I'll try to remember it long enough to fill you in...

Dec. 30, 1993–Jan. 5, 1994

Poor Pearl Bailey

You know, I hate to harp on things. But, just as Christmas is finally over, along comes the next most depressing holiday of the year: New Year's. I don't know why it has been bred into us to use this time to "reflect" on the past and make all sorts of new promiss to ourselves to be better people, but there just doesn't seem to be any way around it — unless, of course, you're smart enough to know that this is just like any other day, and there really isn't any reason to torture yourself this way. I mean, why, just because we're ushering out 1993 and ushering in 1994, should we have to give up meat, sex, fur, excessive drinking, and sweets, and suddenly give half our paychecks to charity, be nice to small children, not curse in traffic, and join some sort of horrid organized religion? Why do we want to ruin our lives this way, just because it's a new year? Aren't things bad enough already? Didn't you just have to go back to the mall to exchange all the clothes you got for Christmas, which are all just a little too small even though they were the size that fit you perfectly last year? Didn't you just finally get rid of all the relatives who've been invading your house for the last week? And the ironic thing about it all is that even given all this turmoil and angst, New Year's Eve is supposed to be a time when we are happy. Happy? Can you imagine? I think they ought to make it National Divorce Day, and if you've been even remotely thinking of getting a divorce, you get it free on December 31st. Or National Put Your Child Up For Adoption Day. The brats are getting on your nerves? Get rid of 'em on December 31st, and make the government take them if no one else will. National Automobile Accident Day. Trying to get somewhere in traffic and the person in front of you is driving 15 mph? Mow 'em down, and have the government pick up the tab. These are the kinds of things to be happy about, but I doubt seriously they are going to happen any time soon. So the only thing to do is pay attention to the things that are going to happen. That's right, the one good thing about the coming of a new year are the many lists of "predictions," the milestones to come as seen by the country's great psychics, fortune-tellers, and other phonies who make a living by gouging money out of people by explaining their lives to them as interpreted through a deck of cards, or better yet, "visions." Even some of the country's most reputable publications, such as the *National Enquirer*, come up with some pretty unbelievable things. For instance, one of their top swamis is predicting that Michael Jackson will buy a huge estate in Switzerland, have his animal menagerie shipped there, open a recording studio there, and stay out of the American limelight. Well, nonsense. I predict that he'll become the new corporate spokesperson for JC Penney, announcing that he and the store frequently have boys' underwear half off. Then there's the *Enquirer*'s absurd notion that Oprah Winfrey will announce publicly that she's addicted to weight loss and gain and will have herself analyzed by a psychiatrist on the air. A true psychic would not predict this, when everyone knows that Oprah is going to be arrested and jailed in 1994, when O'Hare Airport police officers lift up her dress and discover 60 pounds of crack. (I predicted this last year, and she had to go and run that marathon and lose that weight, the hag. But there's still hope.) And what about Cindy Crawford and Richard Gere having triplets? They were just a little off with that one; instead of Crawford surprising Gere with three baby girls, Gere is merely going to bring home a new family of gerbils. They're also predicting that George Bush is going to open his own chain of barbecue restaurants. Which may be true. But their lack of local coverage overlooks the fact that here in Memphis, Shelby County Mayor Bill Morris is going to open his own chain of restaurants, called the Chain Gang, and his photo will eventually appear in that little "Chef of the Week box" in *The Commercial Appeal*'s Playbook. His philosophy on the food business: "Crime may not pay, but it sure as hell comes in handy when you're catering a political fund-raiser. As long as they're serving time, why not let 'em serve breakfast!" The restaurant will be a hit, and patrons will leave cigarettes as tips. And finally, as usual, the *Enquirer* has left out the fate of one major star: On December 8, 1994, a half-black, half-Japanese man will escape from an insane asylum and attack Pearl Bailey. And there you have it — things to come in '94, not to mention a list of every tired joke I've ever used...

April 21–27, 1994

Looney 'Tunes

Here are the things that I'm against: free speech, human rights, civil rights, women's rights, gay rights, world peace, environmentalism, Earth Day, recycling, animal rights, bringing Nazi criminals to trial, and multiculturalism. Here are the things I'm for; clubbing baby seals, killing all whales, capital punishment, David Duke, the KKK, portraying all gays as cross-dressers, Democrat-bashing, forcing school prayer on children, and dredging up anything questionable that Bill or Hillary Clinton might have done in kindergarten. Now. Can I please have my Pulitzer? Isn't it a gas? Michael Ramirez winning a Pulitzer for his cartoons in *The Commercial Appeal*. Oh, I know. It has certainly riled some individuals, including most of *The Commercial Appeal*'s own employees, at least the ones I know. But you have to hand it to Michael, and give him an A+ for the best snow job in history. I mean, out of all those vicious and insensitive cartoons he's run in the paper over the years, he picked out just the right ones to show the Pulitzer committee and win his prize. Can you imagine how stupid they would feel if they saw everything he's done? Still, I guess I'm the only person who thinks it's hilarious, and I offer him my congratulations. After all, look at journalism today. If that doesn't make you laugh, then you might as well go join a survivalist camp. Case in point: Have you ever noticed the way Bryant Gumbel says the word "why"? It's sort of a whining, let's-make-this-question-sound-important tone; sort of sounds like "whoouy." He uses this to punctuate what he feels is his most significant observation, no matter who the guest or what the topic of discussion is. Say there's a nutritionist on the show, because, for lack of anything better to talk about, news shows are always doing various series on nutrition. The guest is some lackey from some useless arm of the government, but since the *Today Show* is spending a few minutes on him someone has to show some sort of interest in what the jerk has to say. So here's Bryant:

"Pardon me, if you will, Mr. So and So, but up until now the public has been led to believe that noodles were a good source of vitamins, and now you've released a new report that questions whether they are or not. Not only that, but you've even gone so far as to claim that macaroni and cheese should actually be called cheese and macaroni [very pensive look on his face]. Whoouy?" Poor Katie Couric, you can just see her rolling her eyes and thinking: "I make a lot of money. I make a lot of money. Sitting through this is worth it because I make a lot of money." Of course, it all can't be blamed on journalists. When you have politicians doing things like Senator Alfonse D'Amato (R-New York) did recently — taking the floor and spending our tax money by making the rest of the Senate listen as he rebuked comments that have been made about him in a cartoon strip — it does make the job of serious journalism a bit tough. And even worse than the regular news shows are the entertainment channel "news" shows. And if this sounds insensitive, then pardon me and give me my Pulitzer, but I'm getting pretty tired already of the mass speculation about why Kurt Cobain committed suicide. So far, we've heard everything from he killed himself because he'd lost his passion for music; he killed himself because of mysterious internal forces, and his addiction to smack was only a small part of it; and, my personal favorite, he killed himself because he was obsessed with the life and times of actress Frances Farmer, who didn't even kill herself, but was locked up for years in a mental institution and then finally got a lobotomy, after which she was given her own talk show and later died of natural causes. So who knows? I like Nirvana's music and I'm sorry the guy killed himself, but I just don't buy all this deep philosophical stuff. My theory is that he probably got sick and tired of being hounded when he went out in public. Whatever the reason, I'm sure Michael Ramirez will, if he hasn't done so already, find some way to depict the tragedy in a prize-winning fashion...

February 23–March 1, 1995

Sex with Snowbird

Gosh dang. Voted Best Newspaper Columnist in *Memphis* magazine's annual "Best and Worst" poll. Aren't you people sweet? I was really excited until I saw that you also voted McDonald's as the city's Best Fries and Burger King as the third-best place in Memphis to get a burger. And that Red Lobster has the Best Seafood in Memphis. And that Mike Fleming — this one could be the clincher — is the second-best local talk-radio host, which proves beyond a shadow of a doubt that either some of you have the I.Q. of an Odor-Eater, or that the end of the world is finally approaching. I'm surprised you didn't give C.K.'s Kitchen the award for Best Restaurant. But thanks for the votes just the same. I'm very flattered. Polls like this are indeed a funny kind of thing. The only problem is, there are just too many pertinent categories that get left out. You know, things like: Best Body Orifice on Newt Gingrich Into Which to Place a Rabid Hedgehog. Best Reason to Never See Roseanne Take a Bath in Prego Spaghetti Sauce. Best Reason to Hire Michael Jackson and PeeWee Herman to Baby-Sit Children You Really Hate. Automobile Hood That Most Resembles Jerry Tate's Hair. Best Way to Torture Anyone Who Is So Tiresomely Late-1980s as to Spray-Paint "Meat Is Murder" on a Public Building. Person You'd Most Like to Lock in a Room With *The Dukes of Hazard* Playing 24 Hours a Day on the Television Set. Spot You'd Most Like to See Jimmy Moore's Rug Come Off. Sexual Act You'd Most Like to Perform with Snowbird. You get the idea. Somehow, these little things got overlooked. And there are more. So I've decided to do up a little ballot, and fill in my votes. Here's a little sampling:

• Best Reason to Live on the River: So you can tell people to drop in.
• Best Reasons for Monkeys at the Memphis Zoo to Perform Fellatio on Themselves: Because they can.
• Best Reason to Subscribe to *Memphis* Magazine: So I'll look better as

72

editor and maybe someday get a great big raise and a car that was not manufactured during a year that I was in high school.

- Best New Idea for Memphis in May: Have the winner of the Miss Piggy Contest marry Howdy Doody, so that her name would be Miss Piggy Doody (a new nickname for your mother-in-law, as well).
- Best Punishment for Memphis Drivers Who Aren't Aware That Any Other Cars Are on the Street (i.e., 99 percent of the total population): Make them stand completely naked in the Poplar Corridor during rush hour, screaming into a megaphone, "I am an idiot and I deserve to be forced to French-kiss Ernest Borgnine."
- Best Reason Not to Watch Any News Coverage About the Republican Presidential Nominee Process: Because examining your own feces for impurities would be a lot more fun.
- Best Name for a Series of Parties to Help Improve Race Relations in Memphis: The Discolored Balls.
- Best Thing to Say at a Stuffy Party to Get out of Chit-Chatting with an Insufferable Person (i.e., 99 percent of the total population): "You look great. My, but you are lucky to be able to wear cheap clothes so well. And I never get tired of seeing you in that." Or: "Could you please pardon me for just a moment. I'm going to go over and have oral sex with Jesse Helms." Or: "Oh, hi. How are you? How is your husband? I saw him just the other night at a gay bar and he looked just fine in your clothes." Or: "Hi, there. How are those anal warts? Still in kindergarten?"

I kind of liked that category. And I would write more, but they won't let me use certain language in this column, so why bother?...

February 10–16, 1994

Share This

Well, it's a very good thing that I did go out of town last week, because had I been here, I would have been forced to attend something called "Being and Staying Focused: Setting, Achieving, and Exceeding Goals." Can you imagine? Someone in the office actually put my name on a list of people who were expected to attend this thing designed to create "mission, vision, and balance in your life." All one giant example as to why people commit mass murder. First of all, there's a clever little booklet that goes along with the seminar, on the first page of which are numbers plastered randomly all over the page. You're supposed to find them in sequence and circle them as fast as you can. I wouldn't recommend this to anyone prone to motion sickness. I almost threw up trying to find the number 23, only to realize that it had already been circled. What this ingenious exercise is supposed to help one accomplish is anybody's guess. I suppose if you want to set a goal to drive yourself nuts, this is one case where that wouldn't be too difficult to exceed said goal. On the next page, there's some insipid quote about goal-setting from Helen Keller. It does not make mention, however, that her favorite color is corduroy. There is also this quote from an anonymous source: "There are two pains in life, the pain of discipline and the pain of regret." Sorry, but I think they need to add one more: the pain in the ass that that idiotic find-the-number business is. And then the little booklet gets to the meat of the matter: Goal Setting. There's a whole litany of clever bumper-sticker sayings and thoughts on this, including the fact that you should only share your goals with other goal-setters and with "people whose support you need." The trick here, as I see it is, is learning how to spot a goal-setter. Typically, the goal-setter is someone who has a phone attached to himself like a colostomy bag and can't live one day without a daily planner. Or someone like that goody-two-shoes Nancy Kerrigan; doesn't she look like the consummate goal-

setter — she, who no one would have have paid any attention to had
Tonya Harding not had her attacked. And speaking of Tonya Harding, now
there's a goal-setter for you: work hard at my job selling baked potatoes at
Spud City in the mall, make the truck payments on time, lay off the Spam,
try not to break any of my Lee Press-On Nails, practice real hard for the
Olympics, and if any competition happens to get in the way, take the
bitch out! I say, with the exception of the Tonya Harding goal-setters, it is
just good policy to avoid these people. Don't speak to them, or they might
mistake you for a goal-setter and might want to "share" with you. If you do
encounter one of these people and can't get away, feel free to throw up
violently. This usually works when you want someone out of your line of
vision. Either that, or tell them that you are sleeping with Harold Ford.
That is a proven way to escape small talk. Then there is the system for
achieving and exceeding these goals, which is powered by the phrase,
"Don't Think It — Ink it!," which means write your goals down. This page
of the booklet also promises, "Whatever the mind can conceive and
believe, it can achieve." Well, my mind conceives and believes that
whoever thought up this motivational bull should be forced to perform
numerous sexual acts with Jesse Helms. So let me just think "Ink That" and
we'll see what happens. And what have we here? A page to write down
your most important goal. And then a place to write down a detailed
description of the positive sensory impressions you will experience when
your goal is achieved. Isn't this fun. Here we go. Sight: The inside of a bank
vault. Sound: The clerk at Dean & Deluca saying, "Why, Mr. Sampson, this
is quite a purchase. I can't believe you just bought the store." Touch: My
fist accidentally colliding with Bob Dole's nose. Taste: The turkey at
Thanksgiving dinner at John-John Kennedy's house. Smell: Lots of cigarette
smoke in my private jet. Emotion: Absolute elation at being filthy rich and
never having to lift a finger to work again as long as I live. So there. Well.
The booklet says the sky's the limit. Finally, at the end of this mesmerizing
seminar, I am told, those in attendance had to line up, do an about-face,
rub the shoulders of the person in front of them, and say, "So and so, I
need your help." Like I said, it's a good thing I was out of town, fulfilling
my goal of never being caught in a situation where I am being taught how
to set goals...

December 22–28, 1994

How to Wrap a Hedgehog

Thank heavens we're almost there. Just a few more days and all this Christmas mess will be over. That would be a comforting thought, save for the fact that these last few days are the worse, especially for those of us who have yet to purchase the first gift. And while there are some good gift ideas in this issue of the *Flyer* to help out with this last-minute mania, my guess is that the overworked editorial staff of this paper has probably left out some things. So here are just a few extra suggestions to help you out. Looking for something for that person who has everything? No luck so far, not even from the stacks of catalogs you've been poring over for weeks? Not to worry. There's a classified ad in *The Commercial Appeal* that may just be the ticket: "PYGMY HEDGEHOG & COMPLETE SET-UP. PERFECT CHRISTMAS GIFT!" Now, you have to admit, even the person who does have everything probably does not own a pygmy hedgehog, not to mention one with a complete set-up (I'm not quite sure what that set-up consists of; I can only imagine a little house with feeding dishes and a sign above the door that says, "Nobody home but us pygmy hedgehogs"). Just think of the glow that would emanate from your sweetheart when you wake up on Christmas morning and you say to her, "Look, Honey, it's what you've always dreamed of — a pygmy hedgehog!" The problem is, I guess, how exactly does one wrap a hedgehog? You can't very well put the little critter in a box and leave him under the tree for several days, with the intended recipient stopping occasionally to shake the box. It's the same age-old problem you'd have if you answered this other ad in the same issue of the paper: "POT-BELLY PIGS, BABIES, BLK. OR WHT., M/F. JUST IN TIME FOR X-MAS!" Yes, a pig would make a stunning Christmas present, but, again, how in the hell would you wrap it? I guess you could just put a little red Christmas sweater on it and simply unleash it on the person you're giving it to. If livestock is not your idea of the perfect holiday gift, there are other things you probably haven't thought of. There's an "invisible fence" company in town that's having a going-out-of-business sale. If your husband has been wanting to fence the yard in, you could always just say that you've had one of these installed for him, without actually buying one. "Look, Dear, I've had the yard fenced for you for Christmas. What's that? Oh, yes, there is a fence there, but it's one of those new high-tech invisible ones." He's happy and you haven't spent a penny. Or you could always get your special someone a subscription to *Pizza Today* magazine. The editor of this remarkable publication actually called me the other day, and you'll be happy to know that they're doing an article on the Elvis memorabilia collection at Broadway Pizza, as well as a story on Pat's A Pizza on Summer Avenue, in which they will explain, hopefully, how and why that woman manages to sleep all night in that recliner near the front door, with the wall-mounted television blaring, right next to the framed hologram of Jesus' face. At one store in town, I did see a very attractive cookie jar — made in the shape of an animal's butt. Isn't that appetizing. The perfect gift for that special child. "Mommy, I'm hungry. Can I please have some cookies?" "Yes, Baby. Just go grab some out of your butt." All of this talk about butts has caused me to revert to a moronic game I play to amuse myself when I know total nervous collapse is just around the corner — a game I may have mentioned before, during which you sit around and insert the word "anus" into the titles of movies and songs. Here's a special holiday version: *IT'S A WONDERFUL ANUS. ANUS IN CONNECTICUT. HOW THE GRINCH STOLE ANUS. ANUS INN,* or *HOLIDAY ANUS. SILENT ANUS, DEADLY ANUS. THE ANUS OF ST. MARY'S. ANUS BELLS. ANUS ON 34TH STREET. CHARLIE BROWN'S CHRISTMAS ANUS. ANSUSES ROASTING ON AN OPEN FIRE. THE NUTCRACKER ANUS. OH, COME ALL YE ANUSES. WALKING IN AN ANUS WONDERLAND. I'M DREAMING OF A WHITE ANUS. AWAY IN AN ANUS. HAVE A HOLLY JOLLY ANUS. RUDOLPH THE RED-ANUSED REINDEER. IT'S GOING TO BE A BLUE ANUS WITHOUT YOU.* The list goes on and on. Like I said, this only happens when total nervous collapse is right around the corner . . . pretty much any given time. Especially this time of year, with just a few shopping days left, and all those pygmy hedgehogs to get to...

January 19–25, 1995

Natural-Born Disasters

Why is it that we live in the tackiest country in the world? Or is it just that every time there's a natural disaster or some other horrible thing happens, the media manage to capture on film the most astonishingly repulsive people imaginable for comment? Take the Susan Smith saga. Now, I realize that her murdering her own two children was a terrible thing, and not a thing to poke fun at, but why does the media keep interviewing the people they've been interviewing? They keep going out to that spot by that lake and asking people with no legal authority whatsoever what should be done with Susan Smith. I saw them doing it on the news this morning: "Waaell," said a woman from some other state, who had absolutely no connection to the whole incident other than morbid curiosity, "y'know, it's been real, real hard on us, but nayaw God is goin' to have the last word and put Susan Smith whur she belawngs." Great. If I had been the reporter, I would have said, "Hard on us? What the hell are you talking about, you moron? Who are you? You don't even know these people. You've never been to this town. I bet you're one of those people who really gets a charge out of delivering the news that there's been a death in the family. Why don't you drag your big fat butt back to wherever it is you're from, and get out of this camera's line of vision before you break it!" Pause. "For WJGH, this is Tim Sampson. Now back to you, Katie." And then there are all the lovely vigilante types who want to do the Susan Smith sentencing themselves. Said one South Carolina woman who also had nothing to do with this family or this case: "Naw! Naw! Naw! The death penalty would be the easy way out! I thank what they ought to do is to lock her up in a tiny little cell with pitchers of them kids taped aalllll over the walls, so's she'll have to look at them ever minute of ever hour of ever day for the rest of her life!" Well, thank you, Supreme Court judge-hopeful from Hooterville. Why are we wasting our money on the American justice system, when we have experts like you ranting and raving for free? It's the same thing whenever there's a tornado, hurricane, flood, mass murder, anything — again, proving my point that attractive people are never part of disasters. No, disasters and other horrible things only happen to people who are professionals at relishing in disasters and other horrible things. I just wonder if this goes on in other countries. Like in Adeline, Australia, where an accountant recently murdered two of his coworkers who had put a 'Kick Me' sign on his back and let him walk around wearing it all day long while the rest of the office laughed behind his back. The news account didn't have anyone commenting on this heinous crime, but you can bet if it had happened in America, especially in the South, it would have gone something like this: "Wayal, I thank it was turrible that they did that man this way, but that didn't give him no cause to shoot their faces off. I thank they ought to make him wear one of them 'Kick Me' signs for the rest of his whole life, and then they ought to chop him up and feed him to the dawgs when he finally dies." I think you know what I mean. If not, just watch the evening news and see how many people interviewed do not sound as if they are on the way home from a beauty parlor in Millington...

June 23–29, 1994

Don't Pick up the Soap

POLICE SQUEEZE O.J. By far, My favorite line so far in the media circus surrounding the O.J. Simpson double-murder-high-speed-chase-possible-suicide-finally-caught saga. Forget that little fact that we're about to go to war again with North Korea. It's O.J. the country is obsessed with. Here are just a few of the comments I've overheard so far: "Of course, he did it. You can tell by looking at him that he's lost his mind." "O.J. couldn't have done it; he's just so cute." "He probably was just all tooted up and didn't have his wits about him." "I wonder if they're already making a TV movie about it?" "There ain't no way he could have done it; he was too good of a football player." "Oh, God, even if he did do it I hope they let him go." "She probably deserved it." "He's just a maniac and ought to be put to death." That's just a few. Personally, I find the whole scene astonishing. People who ordinarily lead normal, productive lives are suddenly so obsessed with this that they are too stifled to go on. Children are not being fed. Marriages are on the rocks. House notes are not getting paid. People are not going to work. Highways are being jammed with bottlenecked traffic. Crowds are raging out of control. People are rushing out to look for O.J. Simpson playing cards. It is nuts! I even heard one news commentator say that this was a more important story than the L.A. riots and last year's big earthquake. Of course, given a society in which Zsa Zsa Gabor slapping a cop gets more attention than a mass murder, I suppose it shouldn't be that surprising. And even my own little brother and sister-in-law have had to think of a new name for the baby they're going to have. They were thinking of naming the little tyke after the great football hero, but somehow the name O.J. Sampson just won't work now. I'm trying to talk them into naming him Ashford And, but I don't think they're too wild about the idea. I still say it wasn't O.J. who did it, but was, instead, Bart Simpson. Look at Bart's past record of mischievous behavior. Torturing his teacher, his friends, his principal. It was bound to end up this way for him sooner or later. If it does, however, turn out that O.J. did it, they ought not to charge him with murder, but with stupidity. The guy has 10 trillion dollars and he pulls this off himself? Has he never heard of the word "hit man?" Hell, if he'd gotten Shannen Doherty drunk enough she probably would have done it for nothing. And why even bother at all? With all that money, you'd think if he was going crazy with jealousy or whatever it was he would simply have gone and slung up on the Mediterranean and forgotten about his ex-wife and everything else. But since I've never committed a crime of passion, I guess I just don't know what it's like. All I do know is, as good-looking as O.J. Simpson is, he's going to have one helluva time in prison; I hope someone reminds him that when in the shower, do not bend over to pick up the soap under any circumstances. I can hear the inmates talking to each other now: "What's for breakfast this morning?" "Bacon, eggs, and some of that O.J.!" But then, since he'll probably be going to that celebrity prison, he might not have that to worry about, unless of course they stick him in the cell with one of those Menendez brothers. I think the one who wears the hairpiece is probably the one to watch out for. Regardless of what does finally happen, at least we can be assured that Americans know what counts: making sure they are informed every time a celebrity takes a dump, and then looking forward to at least 876 hours of coverage on the matter...

Advice Squad

All right. No more yammering about politics. No more observations about the rich and famous and their hair. No more lavishing attention on Hillary Clinton (for now). And no more gerbil jokes (until I hear a new one). Nope, this has been going on now for more than four years, and I think I deserve a break. And I'm going to do now what I should have been doing all along: helping mankind. With an advice column. People are always asking me for it anyway, and I'm as emotionally solid as a rock. It cost thousands of dollars, but it was money well-spent. So what if I still get up at 6 a.m. on Sunday mornings and watch Andy Warhol movies instead of Charles Kuralt? So what if I dress my cat up sometimes. So what if I've never seriously thought of moving to another city, simply because I can barely manage a trip to the Easy Way without having a total breakdown. That doesn't mean I'm nuts. And don't believe anything you might hear about me and women's clothing. A vicious, damaging lie. Which brings to mind a very common problem among people everywhere, one which is perfect to launch this new endeavor. Let's say someone sends in this letter: *Dear Tim: My husband is normally a very conservative man. A lawyer, golfer, and very good father. But he joined up with one of those "men's groups," and the other day I came home and found him dressed in one of my black cocktail dresses, telling our two small children that everyone has a masculine and a feminine side. Then he began chanting something about channeling — or was it Chanel? — and finally stopped that and just jumped up and broke out into a rhumba. Needless to say, I'm very concerned, but don't know quite how to approach him about this. Any tips? — Confused in Cordova.* Dear Confused: Just what size cocktail dress do you wear? If your big, strapping golfer of a husband can fit into it, you must be quite, how should I say, big-boned. Bet they don't have to tie a bell around your neck to know you're coming. Your best bet, given that you are at least as large as your husband, was to have pinned him to the floor and attempted to strangle him. Oh, don't be skittish, it happens all the time. And what kind of jury would convict you? I mean, he would have been found dead in a black cocktail dress, which would surely overshadow any attention the officials might otherwise focus on finding the killer. And you could always blame it on the men's group. Stand up in court and scream out, "You monsters! You did this! Because of you the last time I saw my poor husband he was dead and dressed in one of my cocktail dresses! Damn you! Damn you !" Just keep moaning that untill it fades into an elongated slur, and you'll have judge and jury kissing your royal butt. So the next time you come in and find him, say, wearing culottes and a peasant blouse, wrestle him down and put out his lights. Case Closed. Next? *Dear Tim: I just found out that my great uncle is a cross-dresser. He's 82 and he still puts on women's clothes and walks around the house when he thinks no one's looking. I think he only does it when he drinks a little too much gin. What on earth am I going to do? — Perplexed in Parkway Village.* Dear Perplexed in P.V.: Switch him to scotch, ASAP. If that doesn't do the trick, humiliate him — preferably at large family gatherings — by referring to you running him on errands as "Driving Miss Thing." If all that fails, then forget about it and worry about something more important, like why exactly you're living in Parkway Village. There. See, this advice stuff is a breeze. If you have any problem or unsettled matter of any kind you'd like some help with, just write to "Dear Tim" in care of this paper, and you can just sit back and relax...

March 23–29, 1995

Hold the Sauce

Well, it's finally happened. I've reached the point where, out of sheer desperation for distraction from the everyday trials and tribulations of life (mine, anyway), I decided to "work the earth." Dig. Weed. Plant. Fertilize. All of those horrid things you have to do to make green things and flowers appear in the yard. And how did all this start? I'm not sure of the exact moment, but I can almost pinpoint it to a night recently, when I went to a restaurant that also offers live music, not knowing, of course, about the live music part. So, after being told that the band wouldn't be starting for another 45 minutes, we sit down to eat. Before the waiter ever shows up with menus, the band, of course, begins to warm up. Or at least I assume that's what they are doing. It's a hard call. Anyway, we order, and the band starts. It does not look or sound very promising. The repertoire of the band consists of old Fleetwood Mac songs that blend into old Steve Miller songs that blend into old Eagles songs. It is an extremely strong argument against freedom of speech. I am even more amused and excited, however, when the food arrives, because the "Chef's Sauce" that accompanies the grilled fish is in a little bowl on the side, and upon examining it, I find that it is that blend of flour and water sometimes combined to form a paste that acts as glue. Halfway through the band warbling "I'm a joker, I'm a smoker, I'm a midnight toker," I hold the bowl of sauce completely upside down, and no tiny particle of the mixture moves. It defies gravity. I even shake it around like a maraca to the beat (if you can call it that) of the Steve Miller tune, and still it doesn't budge. Holding the bowl of sauce upside down in mid-air, I begin to look around the place at the crowd that is assembling — obviously here to hear the band. A couple is seated in a booth near us. The man has on a cap with fake pigeon feces on it, and at least 600 keys hanging from some accessory that is attached to his back pocket. The woman with him soon begins to openly weep. I figure it's because this is a blind date and she is simply horrified at the encounter. Until, that is, I notice that while openly weeping, she is also picking her teeth with the corner of a matchbook. I come to the conclusion that they are probably brother and sister and have just found that the trailer is being repossessed — and just after they'd installed the nursery for their newborn baby. Frighteningly, they do not stand out in the crowd. We live through dinner-and a few classics by Bachman-Turner Overdrive — and we leave. Next day. I am going out of my mind, because Cablevision will not come hook up the cable at my house; the antenna on my television was made sometime around the time I was born, so I am able to pick up only two channels, and the VCR is broken. So — lifting myself from my sickbed where I am supine on a pillowlike ice pack because a disk in my back is bulging and is pressed against a nerve ending — I go to purchase a new VCR. The salesman tries his best to sell me a TV-VCR-Stereo system that comes to roughly my annual salary, but I manage to walk out with a basic VCR. I bring it home, limping and staggering. I unhook the old, broken VCR. I unpack the new one. I hook it up. This, of course, takes hours. And when I turn it on, I discover that it is defective and will not work. I un-hook it. I pack it back up. I take it back and get a replacement. I bring it home, limping and staggering. I unpack it. I hook it up. This, of course, takes hours, even though I have just gone through the same procedure an hour earlier. Voila! With the new VCR and a new antenna, I can now watch movies and pick another couple of channels. I get ready to walk out the door to go get movies, and I realize when I look at my watch that it has taken so long to get this VCR in place that the video stores are now closed. I light several cigarettes at once, and flip to one of the new channels, and am again delighted. This time by an advertisement beckoning people to come to an upcoming "Hugs-Not-Drugs" concert to be headlined by — get this — Jerry Lee Lewis. I wonder if they are also going to invite his cousin Jimmy Swaggart up to lead the crowd in prayer. But as for Jerry, like I always say of someone who's Done It His Way, more power to him. But back to the point. I now have this VCR that works, and a friend does some wire-rearranging so that the sound now comes out of the stereo speakers, instead of through the television, whose volume control is such that just as you're about to fall asleep after *Mama's Family* at night (every night of my life, I hazard to admit), the sound skyrockets to top volume uncontrollably. So the new system is great. Except that it involves the use and manipulation of two remote controls (would be three except the one that came with the TV somehow ended up soaking in a plate of ketchup on the coffee table one night), and now when I turn the TV off, the sound keeps coming out of the stereo speakers. And when I turn off the stereo speakers, the TV comes on, but on a channel other than the one I have designated. And the CD player just comes on at will. And one channel will only stay on for a few seconds, followed by the screen turning bright blue. The only way to alleviate this problem is to stand up and move toward the television, at which point the channel comes back on. So to watch this channel, I have to stand up and sit down, stand up and sit down, stand up and sit down. I give up on this after a few minutes, and try punching a few more buttons, trying to come up with some sort of sense of cohesion between the TV and the CD player and the VCR. At one point, Ann Peebles is coming through the speakers, accompanying the TV screen, which is showing Martha Stewart acting like she really does all those things around the house herself, when you know she has a staff of about 300 actually doing all the work. Which is not such a bad deal, when you think about it. But who can think with all of this modern-day technology out there growing like a cancer (as is bad taste, as a friend of mine remarked recently after entering a house in which there was a mural on the ceiling of a naked angel falling from the sky through flaming thunderclouds, "apparently cast out of the heavens," he said, "and hurling toward the earth"). This is all why I decided to go to Central Hardware, buy a shovel and a bunch of fancy (and really smelly) dirt and some bushes and other unidentifiable plants, and toil the earth like a farmer. Well, if you think I've had a hard time with electronics, just wait until I tell you about gardening (and about the man who stopped to watch what I was doing, all the while digging at the seat of his pants). But that will have to wait until another time. If I should happen to make through the next week without being confined to some sort of home...

March 3–9, 1994

America the Beautiful

Between Tonya Harding, the Branch Davidians, and the West Memphis occult murder case, it looks like America has finally put on its real face and announced to the world that it is really nothing more than one huge trailer park. This, enhanced locally by the announcement that "Ice Storm '94" T-shirts are now being made and sold. It's all just a little too much to bear. Do the words "Give It A Rest?" no longer have any meaning? Take the case of the Branch Davidians. Does anyone really care? And why would anyone be so concerned about the fate of those people, anyway? If they were nuts enough to hole up in that compound with someone who was playing chicken with the government while trying to finish some kind of psychotic dissertation on the Book of Revelations, I say they got what they deserved. And what about this goody-two-shoes Nancy Kerrigan? Yeah, yeah, she "overcame great obstacles" and all that, and finally had her shining moment on the ice and won an Olympic silver medal. So what. Have you ever seen her interviewed? She sounds like she and Tonya could easily have grown up in the same trailer park, and besides that, she doesn't have any lips. I'm sick of hearing about her. Especially when there's the much more convincing question looming: Exactly what was it that Tonya Harding felt compelled to retrieve from her mouth while being interviewed by reporters on live television? She was talking and answering questions and contorting her face as usual, when suddenly she just pulled something out of her mouth and kept on babbling without missing a beat. Did she think no one would notice this? Or did they simply overlook this minor detail of etiquette at the Portland Finishing School and Four-Wheel-Drive Training Center? I bet you anything that was a big ol' plug of Skoal she took out of her mouth. I'm surprised she didn't just spit. And you'd think anyone who could afford a plane ticket to Norway could shell out a couple of bucks for a bottle of hair conditioner. (I've decided that I must be hyper-sensitive to hair styles, because I don't have any hair: kind of like blind people with a heightened sense of smell.) What must the demure Scandinavians think of us? And here at home, well, I'm sorry. I'm sorry about the boys in West Memphis, and I know this is a subject that shouldn't be approached lightly, but is there anyone involved with that case who is not married to his or her cousin? One of the men even said he was married to his cousin, and that it was probably a mistake. Probably? And what was his reason for saying this marriage was probably a mistake? That when two blood relatives marry they run the risk of birthing mutants? No. He said they probably shouldn't have married because basically they were just good friends and that she wasn't very good at holding up under pressure! I'm glad to see he has his priorities straight. And where, one is forced to wonder, do they keep coming up with the people who are being interviewed about the character of the three suspects? "Oh, yeah. I know him. Sure, he bites the heads off live chickens from time to time and drinks possum blood and sleeps with a skull in a trailer full of rotted food and fecal material, but I don't thank he done nothing wrong 'cause basically he's just shy." Well, how nice for everyone concerned. It must be that their dad blamed rock music made shy little "Damien" go wrong. And finally, America's sweetheart Lorena Bobbitt is back in the news. It seem that when they let her out of the mental institution the other day, the cure hadn't taken and she attempted to sever another man's penis. Fortunately, she missed and instead cut his thigh, and was therefore charged with only a misdeweiner. All right, all right. So I'm hard up. Go ahead and shoot me...

October 21–27, 1993

Religion Happens

One of my greatest hopes as a newborn child was that one day I would
live in a place where the hottest news item of the decade would be
whether we should name our NFL team the Hound Dogs. Oh, the polls.
The phone surveys. The call-in lines. It's all so very exciting. So what if
we've finally announced internationally that yes, this is the redneck vortex
of the universe? So what if our team name conjures up images of Granny
trying every trick in the book to get Duke to get up and walk a few feet?
Hey, shit happens. There. I've said it. The nasty "s" word. In print. And if
you're offended, don't look any further. Look, that expression is on every
other bumper sticker in the country. It's on t-shirts. It's on greeting cards.
So give me a break. In fact, organized religion has taken on this phrase.
Sort of. Just today I received — and you may have seen one of these
around the office fax machine — a list titled "Religions of the World," each
with their own philosophical take on this reminder that we live in an
imperfect world. Take the Hindus: "This shit has happened before." Or
Catholics: "If shit happens, I deserve it." Or Seventh Day Adventists: "Shit
happens on Saturday." See, they have a grip on things. Jehovah's
Witnesses? "Knock, knock: Shit happens." Islam? "If shit happens, take a
hostage." Protestantism: "Shit won't happen if I work harder." How many
of you are victims of that one? The list, however, does leave out a few, so I
called them up and got the information to fill in. Southern Baptists: "Shit
happens if you don't put something in the contribution plate." Church of
Christ: "Shit may happen, but we'll be the only ones in heaven to talk
about it." First Congregational: "When shit happens, have a feminist, pot
luck, homeless advocacy seminar and march." Satanism: " Shit happened
on 6/6/66." Pentecostals: "Hmbna Hmbna la la loo loo! Praise be! Praise
be!" Episcopal: "Shit doesn't happen if you have enough money." And
finally, the Unitarians: "Hmm, let us think about this shit." See, the list goes

on and on. And some other organizations and individuals have a keen insight into this. Zsa Zsa Gabor: "If shit happens, slap a cop." Richard Gere: "Shit has only happened to the Tibetans." Lorena Bobbitt: "If shit happens, chop off your husband's penis." FLARE: "If shit happens, you don't have a choice." Oliver North: "I didn't do any of that shit." And finally, Dan Quayle: "Shite happens." There. Now that you know things happen to everyone, don't you feel better? I know I do...

Sept. 30–Oct. 6, 1993

Mystery Date

It's a month before Halloween and already Memphis is getting pretty scary. Not with goblins and ghouls and monsters, but with bachelors. I'm talking about last week's March of Dimes Bid for Bachelors, a fund-raiser during which "eligible bachelors" are auctioned off to the highest bidder, and along with the mystery date comes a special date package. For those of you who didn't attend, here's just a sampling of what you missed, gleaned from the pages of the Bid for Bachelors program guide. One bachelor's message to his prospective buyer read: "Come join me for an evening fit for a fairy-tale princess! We will begin our evening with an early dinner at Cafe Society. After indulging in a delectable meal, we shall move on to The Orpheum where we will see lush settings, wonderful performances, and hear memorable music in the Tony Award-winning musical, *The Secret Garden*. After the curtain falls, a limousine will whisk us away to Splash Casino to tempt Lady Luck and enjoy a midnight dinner." Whew. Who wrote this?!! And how many times a night does this guy eat? And that's not all. "Your enchanted journey does not end there! To make certain you feel like Cinderella at the ball, you will be treated to a haircut and style by Barbara Sudberry of Eston. You will later visit Stein Mart where you may select your favorite pairs of designer shoes." Oh, I get it. He's gonna have her hair done and take her shoe shopping? This sounds very suspect. Not as suspect, however, as this, from another of the bachelors: "As night envelops the city, candlelight and piano music will set the pace ..." Never mind. You really don't want to hear the rest, except the part where he says part of their weekend date will include flying to Minneapolis to "shop until we drop at the largest mall in the nation." Why do all of these men want to take these women shopping? And doesn't this sound like the evening of your dreams: "After savoring the delicious meal prepared by the Gourmets on the Go, you will enjoy a private concert as I serenade you

91

accompanied by the sounds of the Steinway Baby Grand." Going out on a first date and listening to some guy sing all night? I don't think so. Why doesn't she just pay him to drive nails through her eyeballs? And again, this seems very questionable. He's not going to take her shopping or have her hair done, but by God he's going to find a way to squeeze in a few showtunes. Wonder how much she paid for this? Then there are the double-dating bachelors, who are going to take their lucky dates to Graceland, the Zoo, the National Ornamental Metal Museum, and the Center for Southern Folklore. Boy, what fun. Why not work in a tour of the FedEx hub, a picnic at the Children's Museum, and cocktails at Chucalissa Indian Village? Other lovely evenings from these bad boys of bachelorhood include going to Opryland in Nashville, singing karaoke at a Japanese restaurant, going to dinner in Jackson, Mississippi; jumping out of a plane (I'm not making this up), an afternoon of golf lessons, dancing with the Memphis Bop Club, drinking "mystery shooters" at Automatic Slim's (by far the best suggestion so far), and going to Orlando to see Shamu the whale. Estimated values for these dream date packages: $200 to $4,230. This is absolutely the weirdest thing I've ever heard of. But wait. For those prices the women also receive a slew of merchandise and gift certificates for various services, including car detailing, spa memberships, pedicures, manicures, massages, jewelry, flowers, and don't forget those designer shoes from Stein Mart! Gee, if only they had asked *me* to join in this fun. Here's what some lucky woman would have gotten: "To begin our enchanted evening, I will whisk you away in my 1976 yellow Ford Grenada, and will even get all of the empty cigarette packs out of the floorboards and seats. We will glide through the moonlight-drenched avenues of town until we reach the Shelby County Penal Farm, where I'll introduce you to my family. Then it's on to a romantic dinner at the Catfish Cabin in Frayser, where we'll dine on hushpuppies and corn bread, and you can drink as many Budweisers as you want. After dinner, we'll go down and get on a Greyhound bus and head for Tupelo, where you'll receive a gift certificate from Lerlene's House of Fine Fashion and Used Appliances, then it's back to Memphis the next morning to watch the sun come up from the front window of Rascal's in Overton Square." There. Total value: $32.50, and you have to leave the tips. I bet you can hardly wait. But you're going to have to because the ever-festive Bid for Bachelors won't come around again for another year...

September 23–29,1993

Hammertoes and Testicles

Just when I thought I had heard it all — the acting secretary of the Army apprehended at a base PX for shoplifting a "skirt and blouse ensemble" (my, how quickly that one was shut up), a Baptist church giving a puppet show last week at the Cooper-Young festival with the little puppets singing a song about religion done to the tune of the Monkees' "I'm a Believer" — along comes a new service through which at any time of day or night you can get advice about everything from the plot of the most recent *Beverly Hills 90210* episode to constipation to the dangers of cocaine to the weather in Singapore. I'm talking about the new C.A. Infoline, an around-the-clock information service brought to you by the good people at *The Commercial Appeal*. It's free, it's easy, and it is certainly informative. Take testicular cancer. Wondering what, exactly, it's all about? Just call the main number, punch in code number 8254. A very pleasant voice comes on and tells you that men should do self-examinations just like women do when checking for lumps in the breast. The recording points out that the lump can be "as small as a pea," and goes on to advise that you should be careful if you have a child "with a testicle where it shouldn't be." In other words, if you have a kid with a testicle on, say, his forehead, you'd better consult a physician — not to mention a good plastic surgeon and/or the *National Enquirer*. And then there's the "Getting Preschoolers to Bed" line which I really liked because the voice on the recording points out that after a long hard day, the last thing you want is a screaming, crying child to deal with. Duh. It also says that the reason preschoolers don't like to go to bed is because they think you're trying to get rid of them, which, essentially, is true, so you have to fool them into thinking you really want to spend time with them. You have to hang around with them until they fall asleep so they won't feel like you just want them out of the way. The recording fails to mention, however, that the most proven way to get a preschooler to bed is to tell him that if he doesn't get in there and pipe down, you're going to invite Michael Jackson over to spend the night. "Don't worry, honey, he just wants to share the bed. Maybe he'll let you pet his monkey." I say, always go with the threat first. Unless, of course, your child is perfect, as is my nephew Ben, but then I seriously doubt that's the case. Moving right along. There's the special "Inhalants" line. This one sounds kind of like a commercial. It tells you that the reason many people attempt to alter their consciousness through inhalants is because they are readily available and much more affordable than other drugs. The recording doesn't go into much detail, but when you think about it, gasoline prices are down, and any number of household cleaners will do. The recording also points out that, inhaled in small amounts, some inhalants can make you "stimulated or giddy." Large amounts, however, can cause instant death. One of the side effects of this habit? Bad breath. Go figure. One of my favorites on the list is the "Why We Hold Funerals" line, which explains how seeing a dead body helps you cope. It fails to mention, however, that the real reason for funerals is to provide a venue for "professional mourners." You know the type. Someone dies and the professional mourner is ecstatic about going to the funeral. He or she immediately cooks several dozen casseroles involving broccoli and Velveeta and multiple doses of various canned cream soups, calls everyone in the phone book to relate the bad news, clips out the obituary and places it with the other two or three hundred that have been collected in a special album over the years, and then goes to the "viewing" and without fail comments on how natural the body looks. Natural? The body is stiff as a board, is covered with makeup, has every hair in place, and looks like wax. This is natural? I don't think so — not unless you're talking about Ronald Reagan. There are numerous other categories included in the new infoline, but I don't really have the space to get into it. However, I will call the "Feet" section under Health when I get a chance, and fill you in on all the details about "Hammertoes," which has its own special recording...

January 7–13, 1993

Season's Greetings

What with all the caroling and wassail-making and stocking-stuffing and blackeyed-pea-cooking and New Year's resolving and all the other holiday enchantments I've devoted so much energy to recoiling in horror from for the past few weeks, I simply haven't the time to get that one thing done that I try to do: send greeting cards to the two or three hundred intimate friends to whom I normally send little notes of cheer this time of year. So I guess I'll just do it here and get them all done at once and have them bulk-mailed. Maybe I'll get Harold Ford to have a little chat with the post office to speed up the delivery. And speaking of Harold Ford, he's on my list, so I'll start with him: Dear Harold, Chin up, man. You just keep on voting the way you do in Congress and pay no attention to all the no-lives who like to see you ousted. And give me back that cigarette lighter I loaned you at the Hillary Clinton rally. Have a Happy New Year, Tim. On to another Ford: Dear Ford Motor Co., Thanks for helping me decorate for the holidays. While I didn't have the time or the psychological wherewithal to get a tree or put up lights or any of that business, every single engine-warning light on my dashboard has been lit up as red as Rudolph's schnozz. It's especially festive at night. Thanks for all your help. Now, back to Hillary. Dear Hill, Congrats again, and hope to see you running the country soon. However, I got a glimpse of you on TV the other day and you were wearing some sort of baby-blue, flowing chiffon number. Ditch it. If that was even a slight portent of what you're planning for the inaugural ball, you and I need to have a serious chat. Happy Holidays, and give Socks a big kiss for me. And then there's Queen Elizabeth ... Taylor, that is. Dear Liz, You know I worship you for all the work you've done to raise money for AIDS and for laying off those buckets of KFC and Percodan, but those new perfume ads have got to go. "White Diamonds?" C'mon. You do look splendid in the ads, but really, you've got more money than God; why stoop to such a level? Leave that kind of thing to Linda Evans; she needs the publicity. And of course I can't forget the other Elizabeth: Your Majesty, Honey, I bet you're about ready to drain the entire punchbowl of eggnog. What a time you've had. The castle catching fire, those nasty bombs going off all over London, Germans hurling eggs at you, getting caught in that photo with that streamer of toilet paper caught on your heel, and not to mention the whole family acting just like trash. I told you when Andrew was thinking of marrying that commoner that you'd better nip it in the bud. And I know you've been reeling over the thing with Di. They seemed such a happy couple. I guess you just never know. If I were you, I'd go ahead and sell those family jewels just so she doesn't get her mitts on them someday. Take the money and do something fun. Maybe you ought to redecorate the palace. I say, go totally Chinese-modern. Anyway, hang in there and try to have a nice holiday. Fix yourself a big toddy and tell the press to kiss your royal arse. Pip-pip and cheerio. Let's see, who else? Oh, how could I forget my pal Leona? Dear Leona, how are things in the slammer? The holidays there must leave a little to be desired. I still can't believe they locked you up for not paying a measly little tax on those knick-knacks you bought. You know how tres anal that nasty IRS can be. What's Harry giving you for Christmas this year? Oh, sorry. I forgot you'd given up Harry for that woman you met in prison. What's her name? Chainsaw? Well, you two try to have a good new year, and when you get out we'll do lunch. Maybe you can write it off. Letters, letters, letters. I'm already worn out and I haven't even gotten to Jackie, Fabio, and my own personal idol, the person who finds the fattest babies in the world for the *Weekly World News...*

February 17–23, 1994

Five *Long* Years

 For once, I think I am at a loss for words. This is supposed to be some sort of wrap-up/look-back/retrospective of the last five years, as this is the five-year anniversary of *The Memphis Flyer*. If I'm supposed to be talking here about the most memorable events that have taken place and have been mentioned in this column over the past five years, about, oh, two come to mind. Actually, maybe a few more. There have been some great Phyllis Hyman concerts, thanks to Michael Powell at Fresh Ideas Productions. There was a great Ladysmith Black Mambazo concert, thanks to the people down at New Daisy. There was a wonderful concert by Ann Peebles downtown in front of the Morgan Keegan building a few years ago, thanks to the Center for Southern Folklore's Music and Heritage Festival. And at the same time, Ms. Linda Gail Lewis (the Killer's baby sister) was playing just across the way, giving, as always, everything she's got. This was one of the nicer things about having been editor of the *Flyer* for its first four years — my friendship with Linda Gail Lewis, for which I encountered a certain degree of grief, since I mentioned her every gig on this page. When I first met Linda she was married to an Elvis interpreter named Bobby Memphis. It was her seventh marriage. We met at a Holiday Inn lounge in West Memphis, and ordered pizzas and ate them between sets. It was love at first sight. I even got to see her play to an audience in Wales once, and she was treated by the crowd like she was Tina Turner. She's now on her eighth marriage, and it seems that eight is the charm.

And there have been others. I met and chatted with Marlo Thomas, and have in my possession a photograph of the two of us, though I've never shown it to anyone because I look terribly fat in the picture. Just my luck. Plus, it was one of those miserably hot August days, I hadn't shaved, and looked like I was on Thorazine. By the way, she is very, very sweet, despite what that bitter homo wrote about her in his nasty book. So what if she sent back a truckload of white roses because she'd ordered off-white. She's Marlo Thomas. That Girl. She can do whatever she wants.

On a trip to New York while on assignment once, I met an actress who has won an Oscar and a Tony. Unfortunately, time has not been her best friend, and she is now insane. I actually heard her break wind at the breakfast table. A woman who won an Oscar and a Tony. One minute she was recounting tales of Montgomery Clift showing up drunk in her dressing room, and the next she was cutting the cheese in a big way. Although I was riveted beyond comprehension, it was terribly unsettling, and I wish someone would help her.

Then there are the not-so-pleasant experiences. I've mentioned most of them on this page before, but since this is a retrospective I'll go over a few of them briefly. There was the man who kept writing me letters, telling me he was in his 80s, that he sold ironing-board covers via the telephone for a living, and that he really wanted me to publish his thesis on the persecution of the small penis. There was the man who called every day, and still does occasionally, wanting me to tell the world of how the local Mafia chased him into a lesbian bar in the middle of the night, trying to kill him because he'd figured out their numbers racket, basing his calculations on the changing price of Coca-Cola. There was the person who wrote a letter to me complaining about a massage therapist whom he'd gone to see after reading his ad in the *Flyer*. It was a nice letter, and he wasn't being a jerk at all; he was simply upset because during the massage, he noted, "The real shocker came when I felt his erect penis between my buttocks." I can understand his concern. Why he chose to divulge this tidbit to me, however, I'm not sure. One of my favorite mementoes is the letter that's still pinned to my wall, which says, "Dear Tim, Go Fuck Yourself. Love, a Republican." I didn't know Republicans could be so polite. Or that they could spell. And let us not forget the serial killer, who wrote several letters to me from different cities — each one a little closer to Memphis — telling me that he had killed people execution-style because of their crimes against humanity. I tried to find him to send some business his way, but never tracked him down. Which would have been to no avail anyway, because in the last letter he explained that he had killed these people over the telephone.

Let's see. Someone came into the office early one morning before I'd even had a cup of coffee and threatened to beat me up because of something I'd written. A woman called in on the letter-to-the-editor phone line and said I should be put to death. A woman with whom I had never spoken called not too long ago and asked me if I would go out on a date with her to a hockey game. I came back to the office from lunch one day and there was a man sitting at my desk, waiting for me to accompany him to the FBI office so he could turn in his parents as the people who really killed Dr. Martin Luther King Jr. And I got a wonderful fax recently asking me if I wanted to become a member of the "Jurassic Prick Penis Replacement Bank," just in case I encountered my own Lorena Bobbitt. I had to dress up as a clown once and perform in the Ringling Brothers Circus in Worcester, Massachusetts, during which an elephant almost shat on me in front of several hundred onlookers. I also had to be crowned in front of several hundred people at a mock Cotton Carnival event — to which we were required to wear black and yellow, which rendered me looking very much like an overgrown bumblebee — and, naturally, they messed up and put the queen's crown on my head, which was pictured the following day in *The Commercial Appeal*. Which is just as well, since half of my mail comes addressed to Ms. Tina Sampson.

I was approached recently by someone who presented me with a business card that read: "Nothing Can Make Me MAD Enough, SAD Enough, or GLAD Enough to Take a Drink Today." And just today, I received in the mail a package that contained a bottle of "thigh cream," and a heartfelt note from the Prozac Society. All of this, and I am not allowed to smoke at my own desk.

And then there are the public relations people. People who will drive you stark raving mad, trying to emphasize how important their events are. Well, I'm sorry, but I just wasn't mesmerized by the notion of writing about a big-screen TV broadcast of live cataract surgery. Nor was I too thrilled at the prospect of banging on drums and passing around a joy stick and hugging teddy bears out in the woods with a group from the Men's Council. Firewalking? I really don't think so. I'm really sorry I missed the Gourd and Hobby Show that was held some years back. And I would probably be a different person today, had I attended Lakeside's "Depressive/Manic Depressive Association Speakers Meeting," during which a professional golfer and a psychiatrist discussed the wonders of anticonvulsive drugs. The annual Spam Cook-Off at the Mid-South Fair has always been a favorite, in that it so vividly sums up where we live and who we are.

There are some people, however, who know how to get their events publicized without being obnoxious to the point of deserving torture. Like the time a local band delivered a cake to me decorated, simply, with the words "Big Ass Truck." Them I like. And all it's ever taken is just one phone call from Chaps to get their annual Fourth of July "Miss You Ain't Right Pageant and Pot Luck Picnic" mentioned.

So what can I really say about being in this spot lo these loooooong five years, except that it has basically made me a recluse who talks to himself every waking hour of the day and has to do breathing exercises to endure going into a grocery store. Also, being with an alternative newspaper has made me very politically incorrect. When you're suffocated with that crap 24 hours a day, you just reach a point where you want to scream at the disenfranchised. Tell them to get a life. Tell the Native American Indians to quit whining about the white man stealing their land and open a casino or something. Tell abused wives to get the hell out of Dodge if they don't like it. Tell the homeless and the panhandlers to get a job. Tell the homosexuals if they wanted to be treated like everyone else, stop running around listening to Sondheim and take down those Bette Midler posters. Tell the sexually harassed that they're lucky someone's paying attention to them. But I would never actually *do* those things, because there's not a cynical bone in my body.

Let me conclude by saying that the past five years have been a fertile time for serious journalism. The fall of the Berlin Wall, the Persian Gulf War, the election of Memphis' first black mayor, the election of a human being as president for the first time in 12 years, Somalia, Bosnia, etc., etc. And while I've been able to write about these and other things, I'm still not going to give up my dream as a journalist. One of these days, I am going to get to interview the Siamese twins who were rejoined by a cruel doctor who parted them at birth with a butter knife, just because they didn't pay their bill. If I do, you'll read about it first.

As for what is going on around town this week, I think that after five years, I deserve a break. So do whatever you want. As always, you know I don't care what you do because I don't even know you, and unless you can explain to me why that man attacked Prince Charles with a can of Glade the other day, I'm sure I don't want to meet you. Besides, it's time to get back to serious journalism. I have to do a story on Tonya Harding, pointing out that she was a nut to marry Jeff Gillooly in the first place, because he's always going around hitting on other women. Bye now...

August 24–30, 1995

The Seaweed Barks at Me

I've come to the conclusion that I'm going to end up like one of those old women you hear about who wind up living alone with a deep-freeze full of dead cats. Only I'll be around 40. I say this because things just keep getting stranger and stranger. And, at the risk of harping on something, I attribute it all to the heat, which is apparently taking its toll on people in various ways. Take the man who — for reasons better left unexplained, I suspect — has been jogging around Cordova wearing only a red ski mask and black shoes. The strangest thing about all of that being that anyone would actually get out and jog in this boiling Jell-O air. Only this kind of heat could drive a person to do something like this, not to mention commit such a fashion faux pas. And wasn't it about this time last year that a man was repeatedly seen running up and down Summer Avenue wearing only a gold lamé skirt? It's gotta be the heat. Think about those poor people in Millington, where the heat index last Saturday reached 123 degrees, and their neighbors in nearby Woodstock, where the haze of humidity trapped all kinds of toxins in the air — not the least of which, I'm sure, were produced by all of the smells-just-like-the-real-brand colognes wafting about. And what about that Iowa Republican presidential straw poll last week, where Pat Buchanan actually got more votes than Lamar Alexander? Something this insane says nothing about the candidates and volumes about the voters. Personally, waking up after election night to find Pat Buchanan as our president would produce a kind of shock not altogether unlike waking up and finding worms in one's stool. What were these people thinking? They would probably vote to have Susan Smith installed as the president of the Boys Club of America. Hell, they would probably enjoy seeing Pat Buchanan jogging around wearing only a red ski mask and black shoes. Personally, I'd like to see him running up and down Summer Avenue in a gold lamé skirt. Only because the heat has baked my

101

brain so badly. So badly, in fact, that I've begun sleepwalking again. Twice this week, I have awakened in the middle of the night, having moved from whichever sofa I had fallen asleep on and promptly gotten into the bathtub to finish out my night's glorious slumber. Unfortunately, about the only way one can sleep in a bathtub is in the same position one is put in when resting in a coffin. Such a nice way to wake up in the morning. I'm just thankful that so far I haven't decided in my sleep to run water in the bathtub. Otherwise I might end up like poor Martina Navratilova — drowned. What, you didn't hear about that? Yeah, they found her face down in Ricki Lake. (Okay, take me out into a field and shoot me. I don't care.) Part of this sleepwalking may have something to do with the fact that since it's too hot to go outside, I've been watching more television. And, as I've mentioned in this space before, when sleeping with the television on, my subconscious picks up every little detail. Just the other night, there was a movie marathon that included *Chopper Chicks in Zombietown*, *A Nymphoid Barbarian in Dinosaur Hell*, and *Frostbiter: Wrath of Wendigo*. Not that I got to see any of it, because I don't have cable, as I have also mentioned in this space before. But I doubt very seriously that having the dialogue from any of these films sink into my psyche while sleeping could be any worse than that of the local car dealership commercial which features two people in black turtlenecks and berets and sunglasses, trying to sell cars in beatnik-speak — only with treacherously authentic Southern accents. It reminds me of that stretch of episodes from *The Beverly Hillbillies* during which the Clampetts opened their beatnik coffee-house, The Parthenon West, which featured Granny preparing possum pizzas and one of their newfound beatnik friends reciting this poem:

"Blue cheesecake, and a silver spoon in the sand. The seaweed barks at me." There. The next time you're at one of the various "poetry readings" around town, slip that one in on the unexpecting audience and see what kind of applause you get...

September 21–27, 1995

Jewelry Duty

Oh, the ironies in life. I was just sitting around thinking about the new trend in running for present: writing a book. Newt Gingrich has written one (or at least he had someone who knows how to walk on just his hind legs write it for him), and now Colin Powell has done the same, and it looks like his book-signing tour is going to turn into a presidential campaign. The irony is that while thinking about all of this, I got a call from an old friend, whom I mentioned in a previous column — the friend who, for a number of years, always took his bowling ball Darlene with him everywhere he went. When he called, he informed me that not only is Darlene still alive and well, but that she is in the process of writing a book, an autobiography. The sordid tale of her life as a bowling ball, passed around from man to man until rescued from the alley. Then the tragic part about how she was kidnapped, taken to Oklahoma, and forced into prostitution. And how she recovered by learning to accessorize (she was often seen carrying a faux-leopard-skin purse), which separates her from the rest of the inanimate world. Right now, it seems, she's trying to decide on a title for the book. It's a toss-up at this point between *Darlene: Life in the Fast Lane; Pins and Needles: My Life as a Bowling Ball*; or *Darlene: A Round Ball in a Square World.* I don't know about you, but I smell a best-seller on the way. But back to this business about writing a book and then using it as a campaign tool to run for president. It seems that all you have to do is come up with a rags-to-riches, poor-kid-makes-good story, add a few suggestions as to how to make America greater, and then hit the road. Well, I say, if they can do it, so can I. Born in Frayser and raised in Parkway Village, I think I can relate to the little people as well as anyone. And I have just a few ideas about how to make America a better place, should I ever make it to the White House. First of all, there would be some kind of new law to control boxing promoter Don King's hair. It would simply have to be cut. The only thing I can think about when I see him is that his parents probably had to put Velcro on the ceiling to keep him from jumping up and down on the bed when he was a kid. No longer would the American public be subjected to this. Health care: I'm all for it. And it should be better. Just the other day I heard a sad story about a woman who'd been in a coma for several months. Then one day, as the nurse was bathing her and began to wash a certain area of her body that will remain unmentioned, the woman began to respond slightly. When the nurse informed the doctor of this, he called the woman's husband and told him to get to the hospital and have oral sex with her in an attempt to bring her out of the coma once and for all. They sent the husband in, unattended, and an hour or so later, went in to check on the couple. The man was sitting next to the bed sobbing as the wife lay still. When the doctor asked the man what was wrong, he cried, "She's dead, she's dead!" "What happened?" the doctor asked. To which the man sobbed, "I'm not really sure, but I guess she choked to death!" This kind of thing would never happen again. And there are other terribly important issues to be dealt with, such as the death penalty. My advice: Use it, but only to rid the world of parasites like Demi Moore and Bruce Willis. Abortion: If you watch enough daytime television, you probably already realize that it's too late for it to do much good; the great unwashed are already there, and they continue to keep breeding. The O.J. Simpson Trial: A new law would require all commentators to use the phrase "jewelry" when they should be saying "jury." For instance: "Today, Judge Ito had to admonish the jewelry in courtroom during the proceedings." Or: "It is obvious that this jewelry is becoming very tired." Of course, that same statement could be made about anything shown on the QVC shopping network or on MTV...

Sept 14–20, 1995

A Little Dab of ABBA

You know, as I was sitting at home alone Saturday night, listening to ABBA records, pestering my cat about whether or not she should start seeing an animal psychiatrist, and reliving on the phone with a friend the fact that as a very small child I used to crush up mussel shells and make various fertilizers for my experimental vegetable garden, it occurred to me that something wasn't right. Forget the fact that I was actually pacing around wondering when "Waterloo" was going to play. Forget the fact that I tried to watch television but on one channel was that commercial which warns, "When your children have head lice, every minute counts," and on the other channel there was something about the religious right, which is too upsetting even for me to watch because those people all have such inexplicably grotesque hairstyles. And forget the fact that as I spoke to the cat about her strange behavior, she simply walked away periodically and sharpened her claws on the sofa, all the while looking at me as if I had a booger hanging out of my nose. None of this was really all that out of the ordinary, unfortunately. What was really strange was that in the midst of all this, I ran across a newspaper article on "How to Keep Boredom From Getting You Down." Ah ha, I thought to myself. What perfect timing. But the suggestions offered up in the article posed a few problems. One, for instance, was "Get in shape. But don't join a health club to do it. Walk to the store instead of driving. When you feel good physically, you feel good mentally." I would do that, but half the fun of driving around the corner to my little neighborhood convenience store is seeing how fast I can get in and out of my car without being hit up for money, being hit up for a ride, or making eye contact with the man who stands out there talking to himself and pointing at me and laughing. Besides, the last time I tried anything physical, I wound up nearly losing a leg. Not a great idea. The next suggestion was, "Concentrate on people, not things. Get together with an old friend you haven't seen in a while. Talk about the terrific times you've shared, and your spirits will soar." So I tried to call my friend who once filled his house as full as he could stuff it with dead tree limbs and put a sign on the front door that read, "Dead Tree Museum." This is the same person who woke up one morning, read a headline in the paper that said, "Dead Man Found in Woman's Clothing," and read further only to find that the address where the dead body was found happened to be his own address, and realized that the body had been found in his front yard in the middle of the night while he was sleeping. Can you imagine missing out on something like that going on right in your front yard? How depressing. Anyway, I was going to call him and relive some of the magical moments from our friendship, but I couldn't find his number, and I think he may have had his name changed. (If you are out there, call me.) The list of suggestions went on and on, but I knew none of them was going to actually do me any good, so, feeling a sense of let-down after the ABBA tape had concluded, I mustered up the initiative to leave the house, and later found myself in a bathroom with a female impersonator's fingers stuck in my ears while I drank a glass of water, trying to cure the hiccups, which were the result of inhaling my favorite culinary treat, Cheese Krystals. The moral to all of this? When you have space to fill in a newspaper column, never attempt to quit smoking, and when you dine out at Krystal, chew slowly...